EXTRACT

FROM THE LAST WILL AND TESTAMENT

OF THE LATE

REV. JOHN BAMPTON

CANON OF SALISBURY

"... I give and bequeath my Lands and Estates to the Chancellor, Masters, and Scholars of the University of Oxford for ever, to have and to hold all and singular the said Lands or Estates upon trust, and to the intents and purposes hereinafter mentioned; that is to say, I will and appoint that the Vice-Chancellor of the University of Oxford for the time being shall take and receive all the rents, issues, and profits thereof, and (after all taxes, reparations, and necessary deductions made) that he pay all the remainder to the endowment of eight Divinity Lecture Sermons, to be established for ever in the said University, and to be performed in the manner following:

"I direct and appoint, that, upon the first Tuesday in Easter Term, a Lecturer be yearly chosen by the Heads of Colleges only, and by no others, in the room adjoining to the Printing-House, between the hours of ten in the morning and two in the afternoon, to preach eight Divinity Lecture Sermons, the year following, at St. Mary's in Oxford, between the commencement of the last month in Lent Term, and the end of the third week in Act Term.

EXTRACT FROM CANON BAMPTON'S WILL

"Also I direct and appoint, that the eight Divinity Lecture Sermons shall be preached upon either of the following Subjects—to confirm and establish the Christian Faith, and to confute all heretics and schismatics—upon the divine authority of the holy Scriptures—upon the authority of the writings of the primitive Fathers, as to the faith and practice of the primitive Church—upon the Divinity of our Lord and Saviour Jesus Christ—upon the Divinity of the Holy Ghost—upon the Articles of the Christian Faith, as comprehended in the Apostles' and Nicene Creeds.

"Also I direct, that thirty copies of the eight Divinity Lecture Sermons shall be always printed, within two months after they are preached; and one copy shall be given to the Chancellor of the University, and one copy to the Head of every College, and one copy to the Mayor of the city of Oxford, and one copy to be put into the Bodleian Library; and the expense of printing them shall be paid out of the revenue of the Land or Estates given for establishing the Divinity Lecture Sermons, and the Preacher shall not be paid, nor be entitled to the revenue, before they are printed.

"Also I direct and appoint, that no person shall be qualified to preach the Divinity Lecture Sermons, unless he hath taken the degree of Master of Arts at least, in one of the two Universities of Oxford or Cambridge; and that the same person shall never preach the Divinity Lecture Sermons twice."

CREED AND THE CREEDS

BY THE SAME AUTHOR.

PASTOR AGNORUM: A Schoolmaster's Afterthoughts. Crown 8vo. 5s. net.

PASTOR OVIUM: The Day-Book of a Country Parson. Crown 8vo. 5s. net.

SERMONS TO PASTORS AND MASTERS. Crown 8vo. 5s. net.

WHAT IS FAITH? A Hermit's Epistle to Some that are Without. Crown 8vo. 5s. net.

LONGMANS, GREEN, & CO.
LONDON, NEW YORK, BOMBAY AND CALCUTTA

CREED AND THE CREEDS

THEIR FUNCTION IN RELIGION

BEING THE BAMPTON LECTURES OF 1911

BY

JOHN HUNTLEY SKRINE

VICAR OF ST. PETER IN THE EAST, OXFORD
SOMETIME FELLOW OF MERTON COLLEGE

'He that hath an ear, let him hear what the Spirit saith unto the Churches'

WIPF & STOCK · Eugene, Oregon

Wipf and Stock Publishers
199 W 8th Ave, Suite 3
Eugene, OR 97401

Creed and the Creeds
Their Function in Religion: Being the Bampton Lectures of 1911
By Skrine, John Huntley
Softcover ISBN-13: 978-1-6667-3396-9
Hardcover ISBN-13: 978-1-6667-2931-3
eBook ISBN-13: 978-1-6667-2932-0
Publication date 8/12/2021
Previously published by Longmans, Green, & Co., 1911

This edition is a scanned facsimile of the original edition published in 1911.

THEOLOGIAE DOCTORI
ERUDITO, FACUNDO, DULCI,
ANIMARUM EPISCOPO ET MAGISTRO SANCTO
NUPER IN IMMORTALITATEM PRAEREPTO

FRANCISCO PAGET

HUJUS FAUTORI OPERIS
SERO NIMIS CONFECTUM
DEDICAT INTER LACRYMAS AUCTOR

PREFACE

THE title under which these lectures were written and delivered may seem insufficient for them as published. For the enquiry proposed into the religious value of formularies of belief and the credal principle which underlies them, became on its way something larger— the search for a ground of the soul's spiritual endeavour which should be neither church tradition nor private conscience, but should be both and more than both. Its scope was no longer to reconcile two members of the religious fact—authority and reason, church and believer; but to comprehend in one two regions of universal fact—religion and nature, life in the Spirit and life in the world. The continuity of all existence, the oneness of things holy and things common, things present and things to come, life in the Spirit and life in the world,—this one creation of the One God seemed to open to the view, and the closed folds of the sacred and the secular to throw their fences down: the walls of space and time were rolled apart. 'Our eyes behold a far-stretching land.' Across the equal plain thus expanded lie the roads which, we surmise, will lead us, taught by the principle taken in our quest for guide, to some rallying-point of Faith's scattered and disharmonised defenders; and to some meeting-point, where they that call themselves Faith's adversaries, and are not, shall discover themselves her allies.

It may be only another instance of that illusion of Greatness, which seizes every age and every student of his own age; but to this student of our time it does seem that the time is great. It is in travail with a birth, *magnum incrementum*, a new vision of Faith and of the Fortune of Man; a vision to which creeds and their interpretations, in common with all human 'forms of sound words,' are more inadequate than in our humility already we confess them.

For the churchmen of to-day this travail-hour, as all such hours, inspires hopes for the Church or else fears, according to the temperament and the 'measure of faith.' It may be that, in the total consciousness of our communion, the pulse of fear beats at this moment louder than the pulse of hope. The more is the reason that, if for any one the happier note is the more insistent on the ear, he should make report of what he hears himself.

At a new beginning long ago when 'builders laid the foundation of the temple of the Lord, they sang together giving thanks unto the Lord, for his mercy endureth for ever towards Israel. And all the people shouted with a great shout when they praised the Lord. But many of the priests and Levites and chief of the fathers wept with a loud voice, and many shouted aloud for joy: so that the people could not discern the noise of the shout of joy from the noise of the weeping.'

In that intermingling of a Church's cries let this voice add one slender echo to the joy.

J. H. S.

August, 1911.

These lectures were delivered, with some necessary abbreviation, as they are here printed.

CONTENTS

PART I

AN INSTRUMENT OF RESEARCH

I

CREED, SALVATION, LIFE

		PAGE
I.	Is man saved by his creed ? - - - -	3
II.	What is it to be saved ? Existing metaphors to express Salvation - - - - - -	6
III.	A new metaphor, which is an old,—Life - -	9
	What is Life ? A mutual self-adaptation of organism and environment - - - -	11
IV.	This hypothesis tested - - - - -	12
	(a) Interchange of substance at the beginnings of organic life - - - - -	13
	(b) Reciprocity in plant life - - -	14
	(c) In animal life - - - - -	15
V.	(d) In the social and moral life, where the name of Life is Sacrifice - - - - - -	16
	Which must be a mutual Sacrifice - - -	18
VI.	The hypothesis tested in the Intellectual life of man - - - - - - - -	18
	The Imaginative life - - - - - -	19
	Artistic creation of sculptor and of poet a reciprocity of two Wills - - - - - -	20
	Life then in all forms is the mutual self-giving of organism and environment, of soul and God -	23

CONTENTS

		PAGE
VII.	A last witness—the Instinct of Self-devotion	24
	An Old Testament type of the Sacrifice which is Life	25

II

CREED AS CONFESSION OF FAITH

Salvation, then, is best expressible by the metaphor of Life, which is the mutual adaptation of an organism and its environment - - - 29

I. This adaptation is an interchange of being or 'selfhood,' and at the level of the human consciousness is Sacrifice - - - - 30

II. How Creed ministers to this Life - - - 31
Creed as an Utterance of the inward faith, a 'confession with the mouth' (St. Paul).
Creed also an instrument for defining faith by a 'form of sound words' - - - - - 32

III. 'Utterance' and 'Definition' are not exclusive names of Creed, but complementary; by uttering we make definite - - - - 34
Utterance by a creed is the religious counterpart of the act of Knowing, or the relation between Subject and Object - - - - - 34

IV. But Believing is more than Knowing, and Creed is the utterance not of thought only, but of the whole personal experience - - - - 36

V. Creed makes for men's salvation because confession is the action of one term, the human, in that reciprocal relation which is life - - - 39
The Confession of Peter - - - - - 39
Was the giving of self, which is half the act of life - - - - - - - - - 39

CONTENTS

		PAGE
VI.	And was answered by the divine self-giving -	40
VII.	[A question] - - - - - - -	44
VIII.	Peter's faith-story is that of all believers. Our belief in the Resurrection - - - -	44
	In uttering this belief by a creed we make a sacrifice of	
IX.	(1) Our Thoughts - - - - -	46
X.	(2) Our Affections - - - - -	48
XI.	(3) Our Will - - - - - -	50
XII.	The confession of the Creed, 'I believe in the Resurrection of the Dead,' is an act of self-giving. If it is met by a self-giving of God, so that life results, the creed is true - - -	50

III

THE CREED OF IMMORTALITY

The tale of the belief in Immortality continued - 57

Does this belief receive the divine answer which is the proof that it is true ? - - - - 58

[A caution. The immediate aim of this enquiry is to test, in the instance of the belief in a Resurrection, an Organum of religious research] 58

I. The signs by which life in the soul can be verified - 59

An illustration from physical vitality, as measurable by the three signs of Extension in time, Extension in space, and Intensity - - - 59

II. These measures applied to the life which accompanies a belief in the Survival of Man - - 61

(i) Life in the Rational nature.
    (a) Does the belief persist in time ? - - 61
    (b) Does the whole mind believe ?   ·   62

CONTENTS

	PAGE
(ii) Life in the Emotional nature.	
(a) Do the affections for the Dead survive ?	63
(b) Do they harmonise with the rest of the affections ?	64
(iii) Life in the Will.	
(a) Do we will the Survival with *all* the will ?	65
(b) Can the will maintain its belief ?	65
III. The third measure of life, Intensity. Can this be measured by experience, or must we resort to Intuition, the organ of the mystics ?	67
IV We must reconceive the World, and learn its unity and continuity, using Imagination, a faculty deeper than Reason	69
V. The organ by which the soul can know the World beyond sense is Herself	73
She knows the facts of the eternal world by being alive to them with all her self ; and among those facts she knows the Resurrection of the Dead	75
VI. A parable of Knowledge as a mode of Life ; and the application	75
VII. This Knowledge is in part an experience by the senses. There can be a science of faith	77
VIII. Can the Resurrection of the Dead be verified in part by such a science of research into the Spiritual ?	78

IV

THE CREED OF THE RESURRECTION

1. Recapitulation.

The Soul has an organ of knowledge that is neither Sense-experience nor Intuition. This is her Self. It knows the world by living to the world	83
Images of this relation of Soul to World	84

		PAGE
II.	Resumption of the argument for Immortality	86
	By help of an imaging of the world as one and continuous, the third sign of life in the soul, Intensity, can be discerned	86
	The personal being of a friend, surviving in the world beyond sense, is a fact attested by a conviction which has Intensity, the third measure of life.	
	This conviction is not illusion.	
	It is a better informant than Intuition, since it appeals in part to the Senses	87
III.	The knowledge of a departed friend's survival in the world of spirit is of the same order as is the knowledge of a friend's existence in the world of matter	88
	For this latter is a knowledge of relations between him and ourself, of an action and reaction of the two personalities	89
IV.	The knowledge of a friend's existence in the supersensuous region is like to this. We discover relations between us	90
	(1) Of the Intelligence	91
V.	(2) Of the Affections	92
VI.	(3) Of the Will	94
VII.	The evidence then of the Resurrection of the Dead is the life received by the Soul when it makes communion or interchange with this fact in the eternal world—the survival of a friend	96
	This life of the soul which results from her contact with a spiritual reality is in part an experience of the senses, measurable in some degree even by others than ourself	97
VIII.	That a knowledge of the Eternal is gained through the Imagination is the old doctrine, approved by a traditional saying of Christ, that truth comes by the passion of Wonder	98

IX. What then of Intuition? Is it the sense of life experienced in that part of the personal being which is extended beyond the region of sense into the supersensuous? And are Experience and Intuition one same knowledge in successive stages?	100
Communion and full Communion	101
X. The knowledge of the Resurrection of the Dead a clue to the problem of the Resurrection of Jesus	102
XI. A study of a Witness's faith	104
John ' saw and believed '	105
John believed and saw	106

PART II
THE INSTRUMENT APPLIED

V

THE CREED-MAKING OF THE CHURCH UNIVERSAL

I. What is Creed when it is Creed of the Church?	111
It is an utterance not of an individual faith, but a corporate	112
That is, a means by which the Christian lives unto God as a social being	113
Man's life is dependent at all stages on Society, and at the stage of Spirit on the Church	114
II. The theory of ' Christianity without Creed ' considered	115
The apology for dogmatic pronouncements as ' defences of the faith ' forced on the Church by heresies	116
III. This attitude is faulty. Not polemic, but dialectic, is the more fruitful method of dealing with questioners of the Church's creed	117
For dialectic is a function of Life	118

CONTENTS

	PAGE
IV. In the 'marriage of true minds' by dialectic we must regard less what a disputant says than what he thinks - - - - -	119
The Anti-dogmatist is combating not the defining of belief, but the faulty defining. The apologist of dogma should remember that the 'definiteness' necessary to faith must be not in the language of a catechism but in the mind of the catechumen - - - - - - -	119
V. These disputants may be brought together by the principle that Salvation is Life and Life of the Whole Man. Man cannot be saved in his mind alone, nor yet apart from his mind - - -	121
VI. Creed, the minister of Life, must itself be living. What then if a living Creed have in it a dead member ? - - - - - - -	124
Shall we answer that a creed of the undivided Catholic Church cannot die, being the work of the Holy Spirit ? - - - - - -	125
VII. What is Catholicity ? The canon of Vincent examined - - -	126
VIII. Catholicity, as defined by this canon, proves to be Life - - - - - - - -	128
IX. In this truth lie answers to all the questions which rise for the 'Catholic' Christian - - -	130
And among these to the question whether a Particular Church can reformulate a creed and remain Catholic in doing so - - - -	131
X. But can she remain 'Apostolic,' and a keeper of the Tradition ? - - - - - -	133
To keep the Tradition is to keep and convey not a doctrine but a life from Christ, as the Apostles	

conveyed it. The instance of S. Peter and Cornelius - - - - - - - 133

XI. In the transmission of the faith Creed is an agency. But there is a greater than Creed - 135

VI

THE CREED-MAKING OF THE CHURCH PARTICULAR

I. Re-formulation by a Particular Church can be a *catholic* act, if it be an act of life. But how shall it be known to be so ? - - - - 139

II. The process of Creed-making studied in the classical instance, the making of the Nicene Creed - - - - - - - - 141
    The Promulging and the Accepting of the Homoousion - - - - - - - 142

III. *Judicavit orbis terrarum.* A reconstruction of the act of Acceptance by the Populus - - - 143
    This Creed-making was an experiment of the body corporate, by which the Homoousion was proved a truth that brings life to man - - 146

IV. The articulation of the process, into the two moments of the debate in the Council and the fifty years controversy in the Church at large, exhibits a structural law. Faith begins in venture, ends in realisation - - - - - - 147
    The Venture by the Council - - - - 147
    The Realisation by the People—in the Spirit - 148

V. The structural lines of this process reappear in the Creed-making of a Branch. But here Promulgation and Acceptance are fused - - 149
    An example studied; the re-formulation of the theory of the Bible's inspiration - - - 150

		PAGE
	Here there was venture by the leaders and realisation by the multitude - - - -	151
	The resulting confession of faith was a catholic article of belief - - - - - -	153
VI.	The theory of Inspiration is an extra-credal belief; but in one instance at least an article of a creed has been re-formulated by our church -	154
VII.	The case of the Quicunque - - - -	155
	How the Church can so act that her action shall be a sacrifice - - - - - - -	155
VIII.	How it can be known that this sacrifice is an answered sacrifice - - - - - -	158
	The experience of a catholic-minded reciter -	158
	Result. The doctrine of the Creed and of the Warning Clauses can both be maintained—but not in their present illogical conjunction - -	162
IX.	The proper scope of this argument recalled to view. This scope is not to determine the right treatment of the Quicunque formulary, but to show by this instance that Life is a practicable test of catholicity in faith - - - -	163

VII

THE HISTORIC CHRIST

I.	The organ of research, Life, to be tested on the article of the Incarnation - - - -	167
	The Eternal Incarnation and the Temporal are one truth in two aspects - - - -	168
	The doctrine of the Eternal Incarnation has already been tested; it is one with the doctrine of Life	168
II.	It is the Temporal or Historic Incarnation which we have to test - - - - - -	169
	An 'Interrogation of Nature' must be applied to the fact, Christ the Incarnate - - -	170

CONTENTS

		PAGE
III.	An interrogation of the fact of Incarnation in the individual soul.	
	It is the birth of Life in the soul; and this Life can be traced back through all its transmissions to an origin in the historic Jesus	171
IV.	But of the Life in Jesus Himself no origin can be traced. In Him it was underived, a new thing, an act of creation, 'the Lord's doing'	174
V.	The event here described as the 'Lord's doing' is the story of Jesus and its consequence, the Christian character	175
	This Underivedness is the truth which Christians are asserting by some articles of their belief, in which they are liable to confuse symbol and substance of truth	176
	The Personality of Jesus is in part an evolution of humanity, but essentially is a New Creation	177
VI.	This conception of the Historic Incarnation belongs to metaphysic; but to the inevitable metaphysic to which an interrogation of nature leads backward all enquiry	178
	Here observation of fact must give place to imaginative Wonder, the energy in which the Soul becomes her own organ of knowledge	179
VII.	The belief in the Historic Incarnation—that is, the belief that Jesus is the cause of our spiritual life—submitted to the test by our method	180
	Proof that this belief vivifies the heart and the will need not be laboured, but only suggested	180
VIII.	What will be denied is that the understanding can live by surrender to this belief. 'The Incarnate One may be loved and obeyed, but cannot be thought'	182

IX. *Some* thoughts of Jesus are not able to survive. The historic Jesus is not the Absolute, is not the Omniscient, is not the Consummation or Totality of human fact - - - - - 184

X. Jesus was the LIFE In this is an answer to our difficulties in conceiving the Incarnation - - - - - - 185

XI And, among these, to the difficulty raised by the speculation that Jesus was the dupe of apocalyptic illusions - - - - - - 187

XII. A belief in a historic Incarnation is not only possible : it is even necessary to a belief in an eternal and mystical - - - - - 190

XIII. The Historic Incarnation is the Sacrament that enables faith - - - - - - - 192

VIII

AN APPEAL TO THOSE WITHIN AND THOSE WITHOUT

Recapitulation of the argument - - - - 195

Creed is an instrument of salvation, that is, of the soul's life. This life, as all other, is an interchange of Self, or mutual sacrifice, between Creator and Creature ; and the confession of a creed is instrumental by enabling the believer to make that self-surrender of his personality, in thought, affection, and action, which is one half the act of life. If the divine response is made by a vitality experienced in the human personality, then the reciprocation has happened, the man has life, and his creed is true - - 197

But Creed which thus ministers life must be itself alive. That is, its language must be and must continue such as to start the life-movement in the confessor's soul. But the language of a creed, like all language of men, is liable to decay and death - - - - - - - 198

AN APPEAL TO THOSE WITHIN

PAGE

I. If these premises are established, what is to be done as concerns faith and practice ?

In practice very little. The plea sometimes heard for the abrogation of creeds as antiquated and inconvenient must be disallowed, in the name of Catholicity.

Decay, if found in credal language, can be repaired by Interpretation, which is a Catholic remedy - - - - - - - -   199

II. In faith, however, there is much to be done.

Our principles are a call to sacrifice—the sacrifice of Thought, which is part of Self - - -   201

It was by a sacrifice, or passion, that our fathers, and latest the Tractarians, attained the thought about the Creeds which they committed to us. By a sacrifice, or passion, we must maintain the faith delivered to us - - - -   202

This sacrifice may be the surrender of the thought, that to suffer any change in a creed of the individual Church is to corrupt the Tradition - -   203

But the Tradition is not a word but a power, not a doctrine but a Life from Christ ; it is the conveyance of the eternal Sacrifice or Passion -   203

III. A Passion can be conveyed only by a passioning, a sacrifice only by a continual offering.

God demands from the Church, though he may forgo, the sacrifice of the first-born. She must hold her creed in the spirit of sacrificer - -   204

IV. But the sacrifice of Thought must be the Answered Sacrifice which brings life to the offerer; and the life of Thought, which is a reciprocity between subjective and objective, must in religious thought

be an interchange and inter-dependence of the historic and the experiential knowledge of Christ, a 'mutual faith' of dogmatist and idealist - - - - - - - -	205
V. Life, as a ground of authority in religion, is further commended by its power to promote catholic Unity.	
In the Church of England (where lies Christendom's best hope of re-union) Life is the bond of Catholic, Evangelical, and Liberal minds -	207
The bearing of this on the Vestments controversy and others - - - - - - -	209
VI. 'No new Commandment' - - - - -	209
VII. Is Life too precarious a principle to be trusted in practice? Life the most precarious of things is the most stable. The Church was rightly likened to a Ship - - - - -	210

AN APPEAL TO THOSE WITHOUT

VIII Faith is not Obscurantism; for we believers are scientists in our belief - - - -	211
Nor Asceticism; for the Gospel message is a Passion, or surrender of the personal self to the Divine Personality, who wills that man shall suffer, and also that he shall enjoy.	
Nor Devotionalism; nor Ecclesiasticism;	
Nor Unreality; for the Christian doctrine is that Sacrifice is the law of Life; and all nature attests the realness of this law - - -	213
IX. The appeal of this Gospel is also to the Poor, *i.e.* the Many.	
The 'Idle Rich.' What they 'ignorantly worship that declare we to them'—life through sacrifice - - - - - - - -	215

CONTENTS

	PAGE
X. The Rich in Opportunity. Their freedom through service	217
XI. The Poor in this world's wealth. An appeal to be neither worldly, nor other-worldly, but whole-worldly	218
XII. A last word.	
'Life' is as real as it is mystical. If it seems indefinite, that is because man is both finite and infinite, heir of all things, possessor of few	220
Vita hominis, visio Dei. But the Life is here, the Vision is hereafter	222

PART I
AN INSTRUMENT OF RESEARCH

I

CREED, SALVATION, LIFE

[February 19th, 1911.]

"The God that answereth by fire"

I

CREED, SALVATION, LIFE

JOHN I. 4.—"The life was the light of men"

I

A POET of the last generation, whose gift of pungency in the portrayal of the stronger human emotions is perhaps unsurpassed, has drawn the portrait of the passion of hate, as it can work in the heart of men under religious vows. A monk soliloquising in a Spanish cloister ejects the venom of his spirit at a brother monk, whose piety and harmlessness have made him the 'heart's abhorrence' of the other. The climax of petty malevolences is reached in the resolve to gratify spite by foul practice on his brother's immortal soul: he will ensnare him into some incorrect statement of a dogma. There is, he tells himself, 'a great text in Galatians' which entails not a single but a multiplied ruin for the man who trips on it, 'twenty-nine distinct damnations, one sure if another fails.' Brother Lawrence shall stumble, and be plunged in hell.

The picture of folly and atrocity which the fancy of Robert Browning has drawn would be too intolerable to interest us, if our consciousness did not persuade us that the portrait has a truth to humanity. The truth of exaggeration, indeed of caricature. But caricature renders a service to truth. This horrific picture bites upon the intelligence, and leaves stamped on it an attitude of the religious mind which is no fancy but a fact, and in religious life and thought a very ruling fact. It is the opinion that a man's salvation depends on the correct confession of a creed. The ignorant and brutalised religionist of the Spanish cloister presses that opinion to a conclusion which is monstrous; but Christians whom his inferences revolt could not quite disown his premises. His error is in spirit not in logic, and it is not their logic but their spirit which abhors his reasoning. For they, too, hold that a man is saved by the rightness of his creed, though they do not reason that to trip will earn damnation.

Is it not so? What is the assumption which underlies the controversy arising in the press or elsewhere when the member of any Church is charged with interpreting falsely some point of its doctrine? What is implied in the challenge usually uttered on such occasions by some man of law or business, that the questioner of an article of his Church's belief should, if he holds office in it, retire from that office, as an honest man who keeps his contracts? What is understood by the ordinary layman, I do not say of the wiser sort, when he assents to those phrases of a creed which warn him that men are saved by holding the

Catholic faith, and instruct him that the faith which they must hold is made up of the intellectual definitions of the Godhead which follow thereupon? What is the most actuating idea—I do not say the most valuable—of our Church's claim for denominational and definite teaching in her schools, if not that faith cometh by hearing and hearing by the word of God, and that it is in the formularies of a Church that this word of God is communicated and faith imparted to the hearers? What is commonly understood by the 'faith once delivered to the saints' but a system of deductive thought drawn from a revealed datum; and what by the 'tradition' of this 'deposit of faith' (as it is called) but the safeguarding and conveyance of that system in a documentary form? Is not the practice of tests and subscriptions supposed to rest upon the principle that a man's expression of his faith is a voucher for its reality? And, to end with the instance which is most poignant, why do we praise the martyr? Why should a man die for his opinions unless because 'man's word is God in man,' and to deny God in word is to reject Him in fact?

To ask these questions is to become conscious that the attitude we have ascribed to the general mind of Christians, the opinion, namely, that a man's salvation depends on the correctness of his confession of a creed, is a fact. This is how Christians think, or at least suppose themselves to think. If their thought is put before them in the bare shape, that a man is saved by the creed he recites, they make reservations :

they recall the phrase of the Quicunque, 'they that have *done* good ... they that have *done* evil,' shall go into life, into fire. They recount God's uncovenanted mercies, they remember that He looketh on the heart, that His 'larger other eyes than ours' make allowance for us all. But they hold these two thoughts, God's requirement of a creed and God's allowance of the good man with a faulty creed, as diverse and unreconciled elements in their conception of the final fact, the salvation or loss of soul. The religious Populus does think, with whatever correction by the Clerus or its own deeper-minded members, that a man's creed is the faith which saves him.

II

This theory we are to examine. We will not allow ourselves to bias the enquiry by a prejudice against an opinion, which at the outset provokes in a modern thinker an instinctive antagonism. So strong and stately a conception it would be childish to credit with mere fallaciousness. How can the martyrs have been simply wrong? Yet they are asseverators of the idea that 'the word is the man,' and that 'man's word is God in man.' Doubtless we have before us one of those first thoughts of men which are better than his second thoughts, though only so when they return to him as the third thoughts 'which are a riper first'; one of those instincts which criticism will dissolve only to crystallise again in a more intelligent and more authoritative instinct. 'From the great deep to the great deep he goes' is said of man's personal being: it is the history also of man reflecting on himself. And as the man who comes forth from the deep a naked soul, goes back a clothed and armed, clothed upon and armed with a wealth of personality gathered in the world of the concrete and particular; so may one anticipate that the instinct which has taken creed for faith will pass through the gate of criticism to return again as instinct, not shamed by a discredit but exalted by an interpretation.

We are then to ask ourselves whether it is the case that creed is one with faith, faith which saves. Does creed save a man? Is it so, that, when confession is made with the mouth, it is made unto *salvation*?

No answer can be begun until we know what this thing is unto which the confession is made. We must know what salvation is.

What has it seemed to be in the successive thoughts of Christian generations? To the Apostolic Church salvation was figured as a personal share in the Second Advent, a being caught up to meet the Lord in the air and be with Him evermore. To the Medieval Church the home of the redeemed was a Paradise with a clearly featured landscape, set off to view by the contrasting features of a place of torment even more confidently delineated. To the mystic in that and other ages the salvation of man was the grant of the Beatific Vision. For the Protestant, at least among our countrymen of the middle class, has risen the bourgeois paradise, too easily derided, of a well-lit parlour with idealised comfort, spaciousness, brightness, and socialities of worship. And for the religious of our day who reflect—heaven has no landscape, and salvation is a condition which has no form or feature, because reflection has shattered the old images of our fate, and the new are yet to build.

For images are they all, these presentations to the mind of the fact named Salvation: 'the best in this kind are but shadows.' To remember that they are so is the beginning of wisdom for the thinker about faith; and it is a beginning which some or many fail to make, of those who offer to reason with their fellow-men about man's final destiny. The shifting conceptions of heaven and hell are but variable service of metaphor, such metaphor in each age as the age could fashion out of the material that lay in the grasp of its own experience. The first Christian age had as material for its fancy the eschatology of the Jew, which it inherited. The coarse practical life of the middle ages furnished images of sufficient appeal to the emotions in the feudal court and the torture-chamber. The juridical mind of the eighteenth century framed a mechanic theory of salvation out of the machinery of the legal process and the apparatus of a law-court. The middle-class Englishman, having constructed the good English life of family, remains, as a certain one of his own poets has said, 'true to the kindred points of heaven and home' by constructing the heavenly happiness after the pattern he had seen on earth. Each metaphor was helpful in its time, and was discarded in turn. If to-day we fashion a new metaphor for our help, we may not count on a more lasting helpfulness; though it is hard to restrain the hope that the symbol offered us by the experience of this age has an element of permanence which those others lacked.

III

For the special experience of our age is of a new knowledge of the world and of man, acquired by its organ of the inductive method. Among the sciences which have made a new heaven and a new earth for us in the last half century, one has in fruitfulness surely a pre-eminence : it is the science which is interpreting to us the phenomena grouped under the once vague, though eloquent, name of Life. To know what life is and how man may wield its forces to his advancement is the conquest, so far as we have conquered here, which has most enriched the dominions of man the mortal, to whom life is given, as the Roman poet notes, 'for all in tenancy, as a freehold for none.'

Life is the category of existence under which fall in every age man's most urgent concerns. In our age it is also the name of his highest achievement in discovery. In no quarter, then, can we look with so much hope for the metaphor by which we may helpfully present to our consciousness the knowledge obtained from whatever source divine or human, of our destiny in the world of things. This metaphor of Life it is proposed to adopt in our enquiry concerning the soul. We offer the hypothesis that Salvation is Life, that to be saved is no more and no less than this—to be alive and not to die.

It is only a metaphor, like those others which have preceded it and are now obsolete, and like them it is doomed, we must suppose, to obsolescence. But meanwhile it is for our age the best metaphor, the nearest to the unnameable, unknowable reality which it symbolises, and therefore the surest 'guide of our dark steps' in the journey of soul along the way of salvation. For a guide we believe it to be. If life be a metaphor, a shadow of the true, like all the rest; if it be symbol and outward sign of the unseen reality; yet it is an *efficax signum*, having a gift of truth, a symbol which is in word but also in power. For we trust to show presently that this metaphor is more than an illustration of things otherwise learned; that it is no less than a method of discovery in religion, an organum of research into the truth which matters most and matters all.

When, however, we advance the hypothesis that salvation is life, and that he who wills to be saved wills to live, it will be said that this is nothing new, but that life is an old and perhaps the oldest name for salvation. There is no need to cite the authorities,— Moses setting before the people life and death for their choice, Jesus declaring Himself the resurrection and the life, the Rabbi asking of Him the way to enter into life, Paul and John and every preacher since calling their disciples to live unto God in Christ. Life surely has been man's name for salvation in all his times : here is the oldest metaphor, not a new one.

It is so. But men, who knew that salvation was life, have not known what life was; have not at least known it as we are coming to know it. When Paul wrote of a 'life hid with Christ in God' and of 'Christ who is our life,' he makes allusion to an experience which every hearer might possess, but none had learned to analyse. There was an intuition of life, not yet a science. This we are beginning to have. To be alive is no longer a thing we can feel, it is already a thing we can describe, and that with a growing exactness. It was something to learn, before the days of the evolution theory, that a living organism is that which has the powers of nutrition, growth and reproduction. It was much more to learn half a century ago from the physiologists that life is the self-adjustment of the living thing to its environment. But we shall ask to be allowed a further advance. We would go beyond that definition of life as an accommodation of organism to environment, and would define the life-phenomenon as an accommodation at once of the creature which lives to its encompassment in which it lives, *and* of that encompassment to the living creature. An adjustment of environment and organism which is mutual, an action and reaction from each side to the other, an infinitely subtle and ultimately unimaginable movement of a reciprocity between that which makes and that which is made alive—this is the conception of the fact, Life, which we propose as the metaphor by which we would interpret the salvation of a soul.

IV

The conception can have no power to interpret anything unless it is the conception of a reality. This hypothesis, that the law by which living things have their life is an interchange and reciprocal action of the two factors, an organism and its world, must be justified by a study of the facts. Of these, some are in the province of the physiologist, as the phenomena of life in protoplasm, vegetable, and animal; and one who is no student of that science must be informed by those who are. But of life in its more elaborated forms, the life of man's emotional and mental nature, of man as a social being and a moral, an enquirer who is no physiologist may venture to speak out of his own observation. And since Life in all its degrees and phases is one thing, this enquirer will confidently expect that his study of the higher manifestations will yield him as fruit the same principles as the scientist gathers from the lower : either study may borrow light from either; the investigator of man's spiritual fortune may catch a glimpse of the truth he needs in the uniformities of existence where consciousness has not yet dawned; and the collector of physical details at the root of the tree of life may find (who knows?) the generalisations he craves for shadowed down to him from the blossom and fruit on the branches overhead.

We will endeavour, then, to justify our hypothesis.

CREED, SALVATION, LIFE

The beginning should be where life began, in time though not in idea, at the point where first matter is alive; or if not quite so early as the very first stirrings of protoplasm (since actual beginnings are too fine for use in illustration), at the point where there is a clear dawn of vitality in those atomic entities, which we call living creatures by some stretch, being more truly the bricks out of which a creature can be built. Of these beginnings of life I read that—

'Two, three, or more Amœbæ approach each other, partially coalesce, and remain united for some time. They then separate again. No new creatures are formed by this contact: there are no visible results at all. But that something which is for the advantage of the organisms takes place during this period of union is certain, and in the light of what is known of processes in other organisms we can make a very good guess at what this something is. Each Amœba parts with some of its chromatin (*i.e.* the 'hereditary element' or 'selfhood substance of the cell')—parts with some of this to some others and receives an equivalent in exchange. The creature is thus reconstituted.'* That is, as I understand it, each amœba has vitalised itself by an interchange of its 'selfhood' with the environment, at a particular point of that environment, namely another amœba with which it has contact.

At this stage of being, then, vitality appears as the result of an interchange of substance, a reciprocity

* Rollestone, *Parallel Paths*, p. 47.

of action, between an organism and something in its environment, in this case a similar organism. There is enhanced vitality, one is told, but no reproduction : 'no new creature is formed.' That higher manifestation, the birth of a new individual, becomes more sensible to us in the range of existence above the microscopic, where a new plant comes into being by the fusion of two cells physiologically different, though originating in the same organism; or, when the zone of sexuality in plant life is reached, by an interchange between male and female in one kind. For each member of the pair there is in the act of generation a reciprocity between itself and the Other than Self or environing existence, effected at that point of the environment which is constituted by its mate. The humble-bee mediating life unconsciously by the pollen dust it conveys from anther to pistil of the clover, may serve as familiar type to interpret the marriage of the Self with the Other than Self, which from Nature's lowest range to highest is her way of creation.

Then when the new life has from such a marriage entered the shores of light, how does it there maintain itself but by a perpetuation of this same marriage of Self and Other? The tree that springs from the reciprocation of two germs lives on and grows by reciprocation with its world, the water its roots drink from the soil, the gases its fibres suck from the air. It is give and take between Nature and her child. The leaf, when the sunbeam touches it, absorbs from the atmosphere certain elements which nourish it, but can only so feed itself if at the same time it can breathe out from its tissues another element of air. Its roots draw up the mould for nourishment, and its branches drop to the ground their burden of leaves which will presently be earth of earth again. Its elastic stem and liquid branches consent to the law of the winds which would break what will not bend; its diving or spreading roots are at accord with the laws of gravitation and balance; its pores and veins over all its frame are of one will with the sunlight, to inhale its vibrations and respire. All this life is union and interchange and consentaneity. Let that interchange be arrested by any cause, let the green tree be severed from her context of nature, the passages of the commerce between them be blocked by cold or drought, and the spire of verdure is presently a blanched skeleton among the living woods.

We can spare ourself the illustration of our principle in the zone of animal existence, because the law of reciprocal self-impartment is not less but more obvious in this region, whether the aspect contemplated be the reproduction of life or the maintenance of the individual 'selfhood' in face of nature's forces—her heat and cold, moisture or drought, the need of nourishment, exercise, and rest. The animal perpetuates its kind, as does the plant; and supports its several subsistence by the same give and take between the matter of the organism and the brute matter which presses on the organic to nourish it or to strain. One passes on up the stairway of Being to where it climbs more steeply in that flight of degrees, the intellectual, social, and moral relations of the species Man that hath Reason, which are the culmination at least of terrestrial existence.

V

And here too we must economise by selection, and make our choice of illustration fall on the less likely fields. Thus to convince of the reciprocity of unit and whole in the social life would be to force a door of conviction that is open. No one needs persuading that the life of wedded love subsists by a reciprocation of love, or the parental love, though with less equality between the terms: that friendship is the mutuality of one with one, patriotism of one with many. The moral life is the just interaction of the individual self and the corporate self, till that corporate being becomes the All-Being, and morality loses itself in religion. It is almost idle to illustrate our thesis in life of this order. But this it will not be idle to remark—that when the stage of the moral and social relations has been reached, our hypothesis receives a sudden enrichment of meaning. Hitherto this interchange between organism and environment has been a statement of abstract and almost mathematical relations. The communications, which pass to and fro between the plant or the animal and the nature in which it moves, are mechanical facts with no spiritual quality. But when the factors in the relation are the citizen and his state, the friend and friend, the lover and lover, a new light has fallen and a colour clothes the facts. It is the light of Spirit, it is the hue of Righteousness. The interchange between these terms is the play of a moral energy; it is a loyalty exchanged for a justice, a heart-service for a heart-service, a passion for a passion, and a fidelity for a fidelity. Under all these names it is one thing in all the diverse relationships alike : it is a self-imparting of one to other met by a self-imparting, a self given up to a self ; in a word,—the word we must henceforth make the keyword of all our thinking,—it is Sacrifice.

We adopt the word, because of single words there is no other that comes so near to the meaning for which we seek expression. But there must be understood in it a qualification which is essential. Life is sacrifice : but there is a sacrifice which is not life. There is a sacrifice which is barren, which reaps no good, which is not unto life but unto death. There is an offering in which the offerer spends his gift, and the gift brings him back neither gain nor love : there is a casting away of life which helps no cause nor yet redeems the loser : there is a sacrificial rite in which the self-torturer or self-mutilator pleases no God nor saves his own soul alive : there are devotions of self by which man or woman only mews up in prison a nature of rich power to redeem mankind; vows in which a potent self is given as a ransom for many, and the ransom's worth is never rendered back. *Tantum relligio potuit suadere malorum.*

This is the sacrifice which is not life. By the Sacrifice which we say is Life, we mean a Giving of Self which is mutual, in which the Self and the Not-Self are rendered each to each, the organism is penetrated by the environment, but is suffered to penetrate that which environs it, in which the soul is apprehended by the God whom it apprehends. This reciprocal uprendering of the selfhood, this altar-rite which is answered from heaven, this sacrifice met by sacrifice, is what we propose to mean when we use the single word, sacrifice, as the significant name for Life.

But to speak of a mutuality between Creator and creature—does it derogate from the absoluteness of a *creator ex nihilo* by implying some self-subsistence of the creature? We suppose there is contradiction here; but one of the contradictions which lie at the root of all thinking about God and man. It is but a form of the problem of man's Free Will.

VI

That Life is rightly figured, then, as a reciprocation between two terms, and that this reciprocation acquires a new character as we mount the stairway of Being to the platforms of the social and the moral levels on which is found the species Man, is a hypothesis which seems to have been now not insufficiently illustrated, though by somewhat brief allusions. The life of society and of morality is almost by force of the terms a reciprocity, and that of an order which can be characterised more specifically as sacrifice understood to be not on one side but on both. Accordingly for more economy in presentation of the argument, we turn to another department of man's existence, the intellectual; and across the field only of these activities pursue our research into the characters by which the presence of vitality can be known and named. In this field the evidences will be more crucial, because the activity of the intelligence does not seem at a first glance to be dependent, as are those of his heart and will in the other fields, upon two factors and their interaction. Science and art are operations in which we might conceive there was only one operator, the man who thinks: indeed we call the man's thoughts, specially in art, 'creations,' as if he were creator and the material which he fashions were dead clay until he says 'Let there be' and breathes into it a life. Yet if, as we have admitted, even the divine creativeness must be combined in our belief with some co-operance of the thing created, more certainly the human creator needs a creature with whom to work his work. However, it is in the doings of mind that the interaction and interchange, which are the character of life, are least obvious; and here the detection of them will most sustain our hypothesis.

Even here we will use some thrift, and select for more attention that tract of the intellectual where instances will be the most demonstrative, because the demonstration is least to be expected. That will be the tract of Imagination. For works of imagination are those to which the title of creation is most ungrudgingly given, as if the artist were among thinkers the most of an originator, and the subject were in this kind the least dependent on the object. Also it is the products of art which we are most ready to describe as 'living,' as though these more than others had the attribute of vitality. This then should be the area to scrutinise for evidence which shall be decisive, that to live is to be in the relation of reciprocal and, as we now say, sacrificial action.

What is it then that happens when Michael Angelo hews out his David from a block of marble, or Raphael paints the Madonna, or Shakespeare writes Hamlet? Are there here two factors co-operating for the result, two terms by whose intercommunication the living thing has birth? Is there a to and fro, a give and take between the artist and the matter—the marble, pigment, language—which he fashions into a shape?

Michael Angelo said that the statue lies already within the marble block before the artist carves it: the chisel does but liberate what is hidden there in prison. We perhaps take that for a fancy, a gracious conceit. Looked into, it is simple truth in a luminous image. The statue *is* there already: if it were not, the sculptor could not make it:—as neither could it ever be made unless the sculptor came.

The statue is there already. To the making of it come two factors, the chisel and the marble; between them the statue comes to the birth. But the chisel and the marble are not the real factors. Behind and

CREED, SALVATION, LIFE 21

in the chisel is the mind of the sculptor who wields it: behind and in the marble is the Mind that made it what it is. That mind is present by the presence there of the physical laws of marble, its plasticity at once and resistance, which make it susceptible of the chisel: for who could carve a statue if marble were either adamant or sand? But it is also present in this way, that in the raw block there is already existent the idea of the statue; in the marble lies that which a Platonist might call the heavenly original, and a Christian the image in the Creator's mind. It is by no conceit, but a necessity of thought, that we speak of the idea of the statue as latent in the block of marble, meaning that a portion of the creator's mind, his conception of the statue which is to be, lies in that block of matter, ready to come forth and meet the mind which is behind the graving tool of the artist.

Here then we have the contact of two wills, a finite and the Infinite. Man's will and That which made him. And the contact is a reciprocation of forces: the man brings and gives his intelligence of the beautiful, and the cunning of his right hand; the marble carries within it the idea of a shape of beauty and the physical gift of a grain which can take on that shape. Each term gives up its forces to the other, and by that crossing and intercommunion the statue comes to the birth.

If the sculptor makes his statue thus, how does the poet make his poem? His case is the same: the poem is there in the material, waiting to be liberated. The poet's marble is the language, with its laws of sound, the rhythm, the rhyme, the melody of syllable and cadence. But behind and in this material there is the Idea; there is the beauty which is in nature, the passion which is in human things, their splendour and delight, the *gloria mundi*, the *lacrymae rerum*, and behind all these the power that makes them all. It is there, but potential, a buried glory, a life hid. At the wedding of the poet's passion and the passion of the world the vision is born. If this seems too abstract to be verifiable as an intercommunion of the two, there is, to help us conceive it, again a parallel in the concrete and sensible process of this marriage. For what means the fact that the laws of rhyme and rhythm and measure, which might be thought to be a poet's hindrances to the making of his verse, are instead his help and inspiration, so that where law is less severe and the impediments less cramping, as in blank verse, there success is harder and more rare? What does this mean? It means that as the stubborn marble grain, which causes the graver's tool to force it, also tones the graver's energy of mind, and enables a more delicate and a more enduring beauty in the shapes, even so the reluctant fibre of the language which makes the poet intend his fancy, provokes that fancy's fertility, yields to his forms a more strenuous beauty, inspires him to build the more lofty line, and so out of the strong comes forth sweetness.

But this, as I read it, is an example in art of the

truth which Bacon perceived in science, that Nature can be ruled only by obeying her. That is, when the man bows his will to the laws of fact and so makes surrender of himself to Nature, then and therewith and thereby Nature bows her own will and makes surrender to the man. Man learns and yields himself to the hard conditions of the laws of soil and weather, and so yielding subdues the earth, begetting on her the harvest: he complies with the laws of water and wind, and so has the dominion over the sea and presently, it may prove, over the air. So at each new reciprocation there springs

> "A bridal dawn of thunder-peals
> Wherever Thought has wedded Fact"

We must let the examples we have studied in art, and those just alluded to in the practical application of man's imagination by the farmer, and by the sailor of waters and sky, stand for the whole induction over all the imaginative field; and persuade us that the same reciprocation is the lord of life in the triumph of orator rising on the wings of his hearers' sympathy, of humorist whose 'jest's prosperity lies not in the mouth' of speaker but in the ear of listener, of the prophet who is null without the faithful, of the statesman who builds an empire by partnership of a people's will, of a patriot Hannibal who fails to build for lack of a patriot Carthage. Can one doubt that over the whole region of imagination, whether this special discourse of reason has for goal the Beautiful as in art, or the True as in science, or the Good as in practice, a study would lay bare everywhere the same law—that Life is a reciprocation of the Self and the Not-Self, is the mutual and interdependent self-giving of organism and environment, of creature and Creator, of the soul and God; that life is the sacrifice made ready on earth, which is answered by the fire from heaven.

VII

The cause is pleaded. And yet in another range of human mind we will address one more interrogation to Nature. What is the meaning of that deep-seated principle in our being, the instinct of Self-devotion? Why do men devote themselves, or yearn for such devotion? Why does Curtius leap into the gulf, and Roman Decius or Swiss Winkelried hurl himself upon the spears? For tribal love, it is answered: but let us know what tribal love is. Why did hermits crowd in the Thebaid, and monks condemn their warm humanities to the grave of the cloister? They sought merit with God in a world of sin; they sought security in a world of violence. Ah! but more than that. Why did Jesuits make over to their General a man's wit and force *perinde ac cadaver?* Through necessity of soldiership. Yes, but also through a more mystic compulsion. Why do our missionaries of religion devote a career to dark barbarians, our missionaries of charity to the barbarism of a slum? For love of their kind they do this deed: but when they do it unto

CREED, SALVATION, LIFE 25

these, unto Whom are they doing it in their heart? The Greek prince, for whom all ventures prosper, casts his valued jewel into the sea. To avert God's anger, we say; but what told him the God could be angry at man's success, unless a surmise that to exalt self apart from the All is ill for man? There are some on whom the impulse to surrender self to a greater than self comes by the anxiety of the struggle to live; some whom it falls on when the storm of sorrow falls; some whom in strange contradiction it visits when a great joy has surged up in them, and in that tide wells up a longing to give self in service even to suffering. Tell us why these things are, or else believe with us that God has made the soul to be one with Himself, and the soul has no bliss, until it can be at one with Him: believe with us that the spirit of man knows in its deep of deeps that sacrifice of self is life.

Not yet, not wholly. Sacrifice of self is not life, unless that Other than Self has joined in the offering: the giving of self must be man's, and also (be it reverently spoken) God's. He that loseth his life shall find it,—else it is lost in vain. The Christ laid down his life; He laid it down of Himself,—but that He might take it again. The world were not else redeemed.

On a Syrian hill-top are met the four hundred prophets of Baal and the one prophet of the Lord. On which altar shall the sacrifice prosper? The stones are heaped for Baal, the wood is laid, the bullock slain and laid upon the pyre. What is there wanting to the rite? Even the ministrants make offering of themselves, of their flesh cut with knives and lancets after their manner. In vain : there is no voice nor any to answer. No Divine One comes hither to join in the sacrifice of men. And on the other side, where the twelve stones are piled, and the wood laid in order, and on the wood is set the gift,—behold, at the prayer of Jehovah's prophet offering himself to the dread ordeal, 'Let it be known this day, that thou art God in Israel,' the fire of the Lord fell. To this altar side heaven comes as priest, bearing the torch; in this ritual the Divine is celebrant with the Human; in this communion the Eternal mingles with the mortal; and there flames between them the answered sacrifice which is life unto the living God.

II

CREED AS CONFESSION OF FAITH

[March 5th, 1911.]

"Words are the man"
Tennyson, *Harold*.

II

CREED AS CONFESSION OF FAITH

Romans x. 10.—"With the mouth, confession is made unto Salvation."

Our study of Creed has required a preliminary study: —Creed is a means to an end, Salvation, and we had to ask, first, what is Salvation?

We glanced at man's answers, the heavens he has successively imaged to himself as the country of the soul. All were metaphors, names borrowed from things seen, to bring him nearer to the things not seen as yet. Each metaphor in turn was good, if it did bring him nearer; but this could only be if it were the name of the likest among things seen; if the attempted bridge from the known to the unknown sprang from the last promontory of solid earth that jutted into the void. Each metaphor in its time might be the best: but each, as it ceased to be the best, ceased to be even good, since nothing but the highest could be stepping-stone to the higher yet. So for ourselves, in the age to which the highest of things seen are the facts which we name to ourselves by the word Life, the metaphor which is to build the bridge into the void for thought's upward passage shall be a figure which is a creature of the age, yet can claim the longest antiquity and the most august sanction as a human name for Reality. Following Christ and Paul and John, we shall say that man's salvation is life, that to be saved is to live unto God.

I

The metaphor is ancient and is sacred, but it can serve us better than it could serve the first readers of Paul and John. They knew as well as we how it feels and looks to be alive, but they had not analysed that consciousness of life. This we have tried to do. The hypothesis we offer of the secret of life has indeed no extrinsic authority; but it can commend itself by the tokens of its accord with reality gathered on many stairs of the ladder of Being which climbs from inorganic matter up to man, 'the roof and crown of things.' We hope presently to commend it by a proof the most convincing, its power to interpret the main problems of man's spiritual experience. We hope to show its efficacy, as, if we may venture the word, a Novum Organum, as an instrument of research into religious truth and the final destiny of man who is saved by faith.

This hypothesis was that life is not an adaptation of organism to environment, which is the most popularised presentment of the facts at present, but a *mutual* adaptation of the two, each to each; an adaptation which can be analysed as a mutual giving of self between the one and the other, and which, as we rise past amœba and plant and animal to the zone of human consciousness, takes on a moral character, till it can be at last described as a reciprocity in self-giving between human and divine, creature and Creator; as a sacrifice (for so at last we thought to figure it) which man offers to God and God kindles by the fire from heaven.

II

If then salvation, to which creed should minister, is life, and if life is what our hypothesis names it, an interchange of being between man's soul and its Maker, we have now to ask what is Creed, and how does it minister to this life?

Again, let us first consult authority. Creeds have from the earliest days of Christianity been called confessions of faith; as first by St. Paul, where he distinguishes the two moments of faith which saves: 'with the heart man believeth unto righteousness, and with the mouth confession is made unto salvation.' And again, let us also re-word authority, and charge the name it gives us with a precise meaning. To confess a belief is to speak out before men a thought that has been the silent thought of the speaker; to make outward what was inward. Creed for us shall be named Utterance, and religious creed the Utterance of a religious faith.

To some there will occur a different synonym. They will rather describe creeds as 'Definitions,' a word which will commend itself to them as having a more philosophic exactitude than 'utterance.' And this word too has strong, though less ancient and sacred authority. The creed formulated by the Fathers of Nicæa and the creed which carries the name of Athanasius would be less naturally described as utterances of the Church than as definitions. Also, it is the word which has become a flag in a modern controversy concerning Christian faith, one side asserting and the other deprecating the use of definition in religion; one making their watchword the demand for definiteness in doctrine, the other seeking for the liberty of the Gospel in a faith which ignores dogma. For the former the value of creed lies in its character as definition, in its being 'a form of sound words'; a *form*, with strong outline and clear-cut feature; and of *words*, whose soundness in large measure consists of their being plain Yea or Nay; a form, contrasting with the formless, featureless, ambiguous haze of conceptions which the theology of the opposite character appears to them to present. Which of these two contentions has the right, or (as may very well prove the apter question) what is the proportion of the whole rightness which is held by this and by that, is what our enquiry will necessarily be asking all along its course. We will at this outset anticipate our conclusions only so far as to express our adherence to the positive judgement declared in the demand for definition, without prejudice to a positive judgement, not declared but latent, in the opposed contention. Definiteness is a most inseparable property of religious faith. Those who are arguing, as we, that life is the keyword of religion, must range themselves with alacrity in rank with those who claim that the function of creed is to give definition.

We are not ready to follow even an Augustine in his apology for the precision of dogma, that the Church has framed statements of mysteries, not from any wish to express herself, but because she could not avoid it [*Non ut illud diceretur, sed ne taceretur*]. The Church ought to wish to express herself, and to express herself with all the definiteness she commands and the matter admits of. For definition, distinctness from all things else, is a character of that which is alive: where the least spark of the fire of life has kindled, something has severed itself from all the rest, stands on one side with the world over against it on the other, says a Nay and a Yea, a Nay ' to the world, a Yea to its separate self.' Life indeed, in one aspect, *is* Definition, and we therefore must readily accept the view that creed, if an organ of life, will be an instrument that defines.

Perhaps one should not pass from our reference to those who challenge dogmatic definiteness without noting a distinction between challengers. One resents precision because he feels the mystery and the glory of things, and fears that any formula will do them wrong. Another resents the self-commitment in thinkings and doings, if he undersigns a creed. In the sacrifice of believing one withholds his offering as too poor a gift, one grudges it as too rich. They are contrasted, as in the life of action are the man who shrinks from the positive step because he knows the momentousness of decision and the blindness of judgement, and the man who only dreads to pay with the person for a step. To the self-mistrust of the one and the selfishness of the other our conjurations cannot be the same. To a third offended one whose eyes love, not darkness rather than light, but the comfort of haze rather than the austerity of broad day, there is due from us a tender forbearance, till he can adjust his vision.

III

To resume. If we accept the description of Creed as an instrument which defines belief, this is not to reject our earlier description. 'Utterance' and 'Definition' are not mutually exclusive names of Creed, but complementary: they are the names of the end and of the means to that end: utterance is the process of which definition is the result: by creed we utter our belief in order that by uttering we may make it definite.

It is easily seen that to utter a belief is to make it definite. In the act of cognition or knowing, which is a part of belief, though not as popularly supposed co-extensive with belief, we distinguish two factors, the subject and the object; the Mind which knows and the Things which are known; and we say that knowing is the relation in which the one stands to the other. Whether or no this dualism is the final account of existence, and if so why the Creator, as He made living things in the beginning to be male and female, made all things to be subject and object and to have their being only by this wedded relation, are questions for philosophers. The generally accepted dualism is foundation deep enough for man's practical reasonings, and will serve for his spiritual. It may not be philosophy enough to reveal to us the secret of the universe: but we are content if it shows us how to live there.

So we take the popular account of the act of knowing, that it is the coming into being of this relation between subject and object, Mind and Things. As, when my eyelid is raised, there springs into existence for me a world of things seen and an image of it on a retina, so when the mind thinks a thought there is created the landscape of an objective world conceived and the eye of a subject conceiving it. Without deciding which of the two terms of this relation is prior to the other and cause of it, or even that there is any priority or causality (as for our own part we suppose there is not), we may call this operation an utterance of itself by the Subject. For in this action, or rather transaction between the two, the Subject has made itself outward. It has projected itself, has held something of itself—something which will now become a thought—out at armslength, where it can look at it as an object, and recognise that this thing is at once part of itself and other than itself. Until it has done so, there is no thought; for a thought is a relation between Mind and Fact; it is the child of their wedding, and, if either term in that parentage is not there, the thought has not been born. This action, then, of the subject by which it comes into existence, the existence, namely, of being in a correlation with an object, or (as we have figured it) united with it in a fruitful wedding, is an act which can be properly described as an utterance, a making outward.

When we speak only of the subject as uttering itself, we are not forgetting that the converse must be true : the object utters itself in the subject, since it equally creates the relation between the two, and in that union neither is before or after other. But, when the matter we are dealing with is human faith, our interest is rather in one term, the subject : our concern is to show that faith knows itself or becomes, as we said, definite, only when it utters self by creating a thought as an object to its vision.

IV

Creed, then, is the utterance which makes belief definite, that is, an object of clear consciousness. But this is not enough to say. We have been taking cognition as an illustration of the process of belief, and have talked accordingly about the utterance of *thoughts*. But believing, or faith, is much more than knowing, and creed is an utterance of far more experiences than of our thoughts. Knowing is a function of one organ of man, his mind: faith is a function of the whole organism, mind, heart, and will

CREED AS CONFESSION OF FAITH 37

together, directed towards the whole of Being in its three aspects of Truth, Beauty, and Good. Man has to live by knowing his world as true, loving it as beautiful, conforming his practice to it as good. He must use a creed to utter himself in each direction; towards the world's truth his creed will be a science, towards its beauty an art, towards its goodness a code of conduct. Thus, while the creed of the philosopher will be the utterance of a thought, his conception of how the world is made, the artist's creed will be the utterance of an emotion at finding it so fair, while the patriot's creed 'I believe in serving my country' will be the pronouncement at once of an affection and a resolve; and even the anarchist's frenzied formulary, that Order is humanity's enemy, is the voice less of an idea than of a passion and a force. And all this which is the case in man's natural existence will be not less the case in his religious. Here, too, his creed does not utter and make definite only his thought. That has been the mistake of the way of Christian thinking about faith which our enquiry is to examine, —that it is supposed we are to be saved by our thoughts, our thoughts digested in a creed. This cannot be right, if our enquiry has so far given us any true results. For salvation is, we are well assured, the life of the entire man, not his thinkings alone : Creed cannot save his soul alive, if it save only the thinker in him, not also the man in him who feels and acts. Yea, let *all* that is within me live unto the Lord. Creed, then, must be the utterance of the whole personal being: it must be able to place outside us, and so render objective and clear, not alone our conception of what God is, but the motions of our heart towards Him and the posture of our will. At one and the same time a confessing with the mouth must be three things: it must be, first, the presenting of an object to the mind—that is, creed is to give us a language which defines our mental vision of God. Then it must be the presenting of an object to the heart—that is, creed will focus our affections on a definite point, in the case of a Christian creed upon the person of Christ; and last, it must be the presenting of an object to the will—that is, the speaking of a creed will be the choice of a definite course of action, the conduct, namely, of a Christian man. The 'Hear, O Israel' which the Church pronounces, to be answered by our acceptance and profession, is not only 'The Lord thy God is one God,' to be received with all the mind; but also 'Thou shalt love the Lord,' to be welcomed with all the heart; and 'Him only shalt thou serve,' to be grasped with all the will. The conclusions we have reached then, so far, are that creed is a definition of belief obtained by means of an utterance or externalising of that belief; but that the belief uttered is more than a mental experience, being the experience of the whole relations of the man to the Reality which his creed confesses. All that is within him must become outward by confession in order that it may become wholly and fully his own, may become definite, may pass from the vague and

CREED AS CONFESSION OF FAITH 39

dusk fringes of consciousness into the periphery of vision where objects are focussed and the eye possesses them with force. It is such definition by utterance that we mean when we say men are saved by their creed, that the confession made by the mouth is unto salvation.

V

But, now, is this true, that men are saved by creed? How should an utterance which defines belief make for salvation?

We remind ourselves again that salvation is life, and life a communion of self-giving between man and his Creator. To make for salvation is to make for life, and we have to ask how creed can do this.

There comes at once the answer, that though the confession of a Creed may *make for* life, it cannot *make* life, while it is no more than confession. For life is the reciprocity in the action of two terms, and confession is the action of only one, the human. But that action of the one term it is: to confess a truth, to utter a faith by a creed, is to give the self.

We must judge of this by an instance; and none can well be more crucial than that of the first Christian creed ever formulated. When a Galilean fisherman cried 'Thou art the Christ,' was it not a giving of self? Did not Peter in that cry give himself to the Reality which his formula sought to name? He gave himself, the whole of him; mind, heart, and will together. His mind. When the long debate in the shrewd peasant consciousness, 'What say I of this Jesus?' is brought to an issue by the shock of a demand 'Who say ye that I am?'; and between the competing conclusions, 'This man is Elias: is the Baptist re-risen: is one of the prophets,' the choice is made 'This is God's Messiah,'—Peter gives himself in his thoughts. For he has limited himself in the sphere of the understanding, has parted with his mind's freedom to do what it will with its own, is made over as thinker to the Fact which he has thought out into speech; the truth 'This is the Christ' is master now of his intelligence. But he gives away also his affections. These are his no longer, to turn them whereso he lists: their object is fixed, and fixed on a Lord who is a jealous Lord; he must love this Jesus, love Him beyond all else, and love Him more than these his fellows, because He was the first of them to confess his love. And, with mind and heart, he has given away his will. To acknowledge aloud that this man is the Christ carries with the word all the course of his actions in all his days; he is free no more to gird himself and walk whither he would; already he has stretched forth surrendering hands and is girded by this Master absolute and for ever, to be carried by him whither as mortal he would not.

VI

This story of how the first Christian made his creed, as we reconstruct it by sympathies which need not distrust themselves, is the story of what happens when

CREED AS CONFESSION OF FAITH   41

any creed is made by any Christian or Church of Christ. He who speaks a creed renders one-half of the act we call life: he gives self to the Reality of which he has spoken a name. Half the act of living unto God has been done, the human half, the sacrifice offered by the man.

But in this matter half is not only less than the whole: it is less than itself, it is nothing. The sacrifice offered by the man, if it be only offered, only laid on the altar, and the fire does not fall, is not a sacrifice; it is not anything. The creed in which the believer gives himself to the object of his confession is in the process of salvation not a value, has no power to save a man, unless the Divine Reality gives itself in answer.

But how can that be, and what is the sign that this Divine Reality has taken its part in the mutual action which is life?

What happened in the making of that first of Christian creeds, the confession of Peter? The follower by his word, 'Thou art the Christ,' has uttered his loyalty, given head, heart, and hand to the leader. What comes back to him?

There can be utterings of loyalty to which there comes back nothing; as when a pilgrim train of Galileans cries 'Hosanna to the Son of David,' and then, under the cold eyes of their betters in Jerusalem street, they find their protestations have been answered by no firm assurance, and they can now only say 'This is Jesus the prophet from Nazareth.' There are (do we not know it?) utterings of our own, which die by the act of uttering; as when a teacher puts forth to learners some article of his faith, not doubting that he is convinced of its truth *until* he has given it speech; and then (for who can be always on the heights of his belief?) conviction seems to have expired with the breath that sent it abroad. These are credal acts that have not saved our own soul alive; they have not found the reciprocation, life has not kindled here. Did Peter's creed find answer?

That is a question which from direct knowledge only two can answer, Peter's self and, in Peter's phrase, God who knoweth the heart. But signals which we can read are thrown us by the story of the man. The life of flesh is declared by the activities of the body, and the life of spirit in saints by the Acta Sanctorum. If the record of the Acta Petri could chronicle no more than that his utterance at Caesarea Philippi opened that train of spiritual consequence which we call the Church built by Christ upon the rock of the utterer, this impersonal fruitfulness of his deed would be proof that here was a sacrifice which heaven answered by the fire. But the tale of the man is not so lost in the tale of the community. The train of spiritual consequence in the believer's own personality is registered with a convincing fulness and vivacity on the page of Luke. We read the brave memoir, and do not doubt that where Peter sowed there he reaped life. The rapture which in the great confession launched him from a brink into a void, did not dash him to wreck upon the stones : it buoyed him on a long flight of spiritual enterprise with wings like eagle's which, if they could falter at moments, yet dropped only to mount again higher. The faith that cried, 'Thou, the Galilean teacher, art the Christ of God,' becomes the faith which at the baptism of fire can avow 'Thou, the crucified, art made both Lord and Christ'; it can lift the cripple to his feet by the name of Jesus of Nazareth, can affront with a follower's defiance the priest who had sent the Leader to a cross, and bear the scourge rejoicing in a dishonour suffered for the Name; can shatter in a morning the race-pride of ages and 'break his birth's invidious bar' for Cornelius the alien man of faith; can be strong to walk in freedom whither he would on the Master's errands, and strong at the last to be in weakness and in bondage and be carried to the likeness of the Master's doom. We read the story and are sure that faith's venture bore the fruit of faith's achievement. The life in Peter was not exhausted by that outpour of its energy, but replenished more : was set on fire by the utterance, but with a fire of the divine Presence which inflamed and did not consume. This earliest formulation of Christian belief was plainly an utterance to which heaven replied, a sacrifice offered by the worshipper and accepted by the fire from heaven, a self-giving of the Man answered by the self-communication of God. The creed of Peter was an act of life. The creed of Peter was found to be true.

VII

One pauses to ask a question, which at this point we will not try to answer. That Peter's utterance brought him life, we who have his after-history before us can well discern: and that makes us satisfied that the creed he uttered was a right one. But how did Peter know his creed to be right, at the time of its utterance, before the history came to prove it so? The question is of the greatest importance to ourselves: for we want to know whether our own belief is true, not years after, when there will have accrued proof of it, but now, when we are committing ourselves to the belief. Years hence it will be too late to know that our creed was wrong, if wrong it shall prove to have been: for we shall have staked our fortunes on it, and they will then be irrecoverable. The question is a vital one; but the answer, if we can find one, will be more serviceably given at a later point in our argument, where too it will meet us with more insistency than here.*

VIII

That venture of faith which stands to the name of Peter assigns him a kind of primacy among believers which provokes no challenge from history. But if it has made him first, it is the first of many brethren. For change the name and of thee the tale is told, whosoever art believer through all the days of the Christ. Is it not so? Would it have been possible imaginatively to reconstruct, as attempted here, this

* This is touched on in VI., pp 147, 152

story of how Peter, one day in a pause of the wanderers on a hill-slope of the Lebanon, sought and found the truth, if his case were not also our own; if it were not that always he that seeketh findeth truth in no other fashion than did this stout venturer, the fisherman who showed the way to a world. The story of the faith of every Christian among us has now been told; for it is the Galilean's story. And yet let us try to re-tell it, in a shape of circumstance and language more new and living to ourselves, that we may feel more sure his tale and our own are one. That our language may be more new and living we will not take for our instance the truth which Peter confessed, 'Thou art the Christ'; for, though that remains the summary of a Christian's faith, it has for us lost the concreteness and the poignancy of human and immediate interest, which faith in the Messiah had for a Jew of the Roman empire waiting for the consolation of Israel. Let us choose the article of our belief which concentrates our attention on an interest not less drastic than the coming of a Redeemer of Israel,— 'I look for the Resurrection of the Dead and the Life of the world to come.' The hope of Peter, 'This is the Christ who shall free my race from Rome,' did not more strain his heart-strings than does with one of us mortal men and women to-day the hope, even under the shadow of a tyranny of death, that

> "for me, I lie
> Broken in Christ's sweet hand, with whom shall rest
> To keep me living, now that I must die."

We shall ask, then, not what happened in Peter, when he confessed 'Thou are the Christ,' but what happens in myself when I confess 'This is the Christ, by whom, though I die, yet shall I live?' When I utter that creed, do I give myself to the Reality for which my name is Christ, the Son of God, and does that Reality give itself to me?

Critics of our religion have told us that our hope in a future life is begotten by a spirit not of giving but of getting. 'Selfish mortal, is it not enough for you to live once: must you covet another life still? You who make a virtue of the eternal hope, are you not in truth greedy men, believing that gain is godliness?' Enough to live once? Why, enough it is for me, who am but one,—if only I may indeed once live. For once to live *is* to live always. But not less than one life contents me; and if it be a sin to covet life, I must still be an offending soul.

But let us ask whether to believe in the resurrection comes by a spirit of greed or by a spirit of self-forsaking.

IX

That first of believers, in the act of uttering his creed, gave up, we said, the self of his thoughts, his affections, his will. We also in this our creed make an offering of our thoughts, a sacrifice of the mind. For to believe that this man shall live on after he has died, is first an act of mind; it is the imagining of the scene of After-Death, the landscape of a new heaven and a new earth. To do this the mind must forsake

CREED AS CONFESSION OF FAITH   47

self. She must cast away those conclusions which are the gettings of her terrene experience, that all that lives must die, for that every sense bears witness it is so. But to cast away conclusions of the mind, how real a sacrifice of self is this! For how strong is the mind's desire for selfish ease, for the peace of a fixed conclusion, the repose of definitiveness. How she wants to rest here and not go on. And what a labour and strain and adventurous welcoming of the unfamiliar is demanded by the imagination of a world wholly unlike the world of sense, in which the mind's home is. Forth of that house and home she must go : naked she must go out of the world, the world with which experience by the senses has clothed her, and wander beyond these 'warm precincts' out into the vast and void. All imagining of that which we do not know, all sympathy with those who are not ourself is indeed a going out of self : but to make this pilgrimage of vision into the uncharted region beyond the flaming walls of the world ' alone, withouten any companie '; to start on this quest of a hospitality for our trembling, dazzled, stranger soul among those yonder, who, however our companions once, are now of all the company of heaven, who, however dear, are in their new greatness dread—tell me not this journey is the deed of the selfish man. It is the journey of that hero of faith who 'went out, not knowing whither he went, and sojourned in the land of promise as in a strange country.' Abandon self all ye who enter, even by your thought, this gate that leadeth unto life.

X

Again the utterance of this belief 'the dead are raised' is a sacrifice of the heart: we give the self of our affections. A man does not credit a world to come towards which he cannot feel an emotional regard either of desire or of repulsion, a passion of love or else of hate. Commonly, no doubt, we suppose that our heart hopes for or fears those alternative dooms of the future, because our intelligence has informed us that they are facts; just as men hate poverty or covet public honour, because reason tells them that bankruptcy or distinction are possibilities. In the doom of spirit this is not so. Reason and emotion here are not as cause and consequence: they are conditions each one of the other: we expect the doom if also we desire or dread it. That hero of a fiction who boasted in his motto that he lived 'ne fleyt at hell, ne fond on heaven,' did not really believe in either fact: his heaven was a picture on a cloud, his hell the place only of 'a painted devil.' Those to whom this reasoning seems doubtful will at least allow that wish can be father to thought, that an emotional interest in the truth is not a blinder of the eyes, but a steadier and quickener of the judgement by the responsibility it wakes; that where we bestow our heart there we are readiest to lay the treasure of our confidence. That is allowance enough to serve our present contention. It allows that there can be a giving of self, the self of the emotions, when a judgement on reality is being framed: and this is what we are saying. In the judgement concerning an after-life, we judge that the reality is there because we love to have it so, or hate. Even of a heaven it is the case that we 'must love it ere to us it will seem worthy to be loved': we must set our affections on things beyond, not on things on the earth, if our mind is to pass beyond earth and set its thoughts yonder. Because our affections are at home there; because heaven is the country of the soul and our citizenship is in it; because it is for us the land of such dear souls, our kindred who now inherit it; therefore are we sure that heaven *is*. The selfish man does not, so far as he is selfish, believe in an after-life, because he does not care for it, does not covet one which should be heavenly; and if he believes at all in one which should be hellish, it is because a something in him, not the bad but the remaining good, makes him able to hate an evil world, since the woe of an evil world, whatever be his imagery of it, is the woe of darkness away from the face of God; and this the good that still is in him hates. Ah yes, our mind gives credence to a world of bliss or woe when our heart goes thither at its side, when the soul of a mortal is led as a bride towards the gate of heaven, or dragged as a shuddering slave-bride towards a king of terrors, Death. Verily we must render up a self to the Reality we foresee, the self of our affections, when we confess with our mouth that the dead are raised.

XI

And the Will? Do we in that act of credence give out of us lastly the practical power, the energy that handles facts and expresses itself in our conduct?

It will hardly be questioned that an activity of the will is a part of that act of credence. We cannot genuinely believe in a future and enduring life, and not make some effort to accommodate our present conduct to the interests, which are overwhelming, of that future. 'Longer is the time,' says the Greek poet's hero-maiden, 'wherein I must please those yonder than these here'; and the measure in which we seek to please that yonder world is the measure in which we credit it: thought and will are as thought and affection are, mutually conditions each of each. Then in the judging that we shall live on we make a surrender of our actions as of our emotions. We give up our temporal conduct to be the instrument of an eternal interest: our creaturely will is offered up to the Creator Will, to work out His word, 'Let there be—a Hereafter.'

XII

What have we done in this train of reflections? We have changed the name and of ourself has been told the tale of the disciple who avows the Creed 'this is the Christ of God—in whom though I die yet shall I live.' The Galilean fisherman, as we tried to read his spirit's experience, did in his confession of the Christ

CREED AS CONFESSION OF FAITH 51

a deed in which the mental activity which conceived the words was at the utmost a third part, and a lesser third, of the whole activity in it of his being. He formulated a creed, the first a Christian ever made. Did that formulation effect the salvation of Peter? If it was only an act done by a thought, and the word that made the thought public, how could it save—even if by itself it could save at all—how could it save any more of Peter than the mind in him which thought and spoke it? But the act of this archetype of Christian confessors was an act, as we judged, of his entire personal being. The heart and the will went with the mind.

And the action of this threefold nature, what did we find it to be? His utterance of a faith was, we saw, a renunciation, a surrender, an offering of the sacrifice of faith. He threw open the gate of his mind to the entry of a truth beyond his experience, a divine thought that was above his thought: he gave away the dearest thing he had, his heart's force of the love-passion, to be a vowed passion sealed to this Christ: he committed his way unto Jehovah as known to him in Jesus, gave it up to ways that were not his ways. Here was all the meaning and the might in the first uttering of a creed: a self was given to God, a man's whole self, when the disciple who believed in his heart that Jesus was the Christ did with his mouth make confession.

And this tale, with the names of things changed into names of our modern experiences, we have tried to tell of ourselves, and have found that it can so be told. When one of us makes his creed and confesses a Resurrection of the Dead, his confession is an utterance in which he gives himself, all that is within him, to the Reality of which he shapes a name.

What then has he done by this utterance? This confession which has been made with the mouth, in what sort and degree has it been made *unto salvation*?

In the language of our enquiry we must say that by this utterance of a Credo there has been done one half the act of life: the man has given himself to God. Half the act. But in the region of living things the half without the half is nothing; life has not happened yet; for life happens only when there is a giving of self not by one but two. Can then the tale of that man who was in Christ before us all, be told as our tale up to the end? The other half of the act of life, is it in our case rendered; does God give Himself to us who give ourself to Him? Is our gift, when we lay it on the altar, fired from heaven? Does our confession issue in life for us?

That is the question which we are brought in sight of. Though we cannot here begin an answer, let us already note what issue hangs on our answer. The issue is no less than this.

If to be saved is to have life, and if the work of creed is to save men by causing this life, so that the whole use and significance of creed is in this, that it causes life,—then, if we shall learn that our confession of this creed 'I believe in the Resurrection of the Dead' is an act of self-giving which is met by a self-giving of God, so that life happens to us, we shall have learned that this creed is a right creed and a true; we shall know assuredly that the dead are raised, and that we, though we die, yet shall we live.

III

THE CREED OF IMMORTALITY

[March 12th, 1911.]

Ultra processit flammantia maenia mundi
Atque omne immensum peragravit mente animoque.

Lucretius.

III

THE CREED OF IMMORTALITY

1 Cor. ii. 9, 10.—" Eye hath not seen, nor ear heard, . . . the things which God hath prepared for them that love Him. But God hath revealed them unto us."

THE uttering of a faith by a creed is, we have said, the one half, the human half, of that process of reciprocatory self-giving between God and the soul which is the life, or salvation, of man. Does the other half, the divine half, in that reciprocation take place: does the spiritual environment impart itself to the human organism, a soul? If it does, by what signs is the fact known?

That question, we noted, is the same, though in other words, as the question, Is the creed true? Creed has no significance and worth and reality, is, as St. Paul would say, nothing in the world, except as an instrument which saves us, or, in closer language, helps us to live. The truth it imparts is simply the life it imparts. If then by uttering a creed the utterer receives life, then his creed is a right creed, the thing he believes is so.

We took for examination an instance of credal assertion, 'I believe in the Resurrection of the Dead'; and were lighting our research by the historic example of an utterance which attained the divine-human reciprocity and made the utterer live, Peter's creed 'Thou art the Christ.' That utterance was the confessor's self-giving, was half the fact of life to him. We found an analogue to this in our own confession of a belief—a specific part of the whole belief in Christ—that in the After-life of the soul. Only by a surrender of the self, in its tripartite being of mind, heart, and will, can we Christians of to-day confess our faith in that fact of human destiny. Peter's tale was ours so far. But is it ours to the end; and does the faith-movement in us meet the same divine answer as in Peter? If it does, then in spite of nature's apparent witness to the contrary, 'yet is our hope full of immortality.' If it does not, then we may have believed in vain.

We chose our instance because of its drastic interest, compelling attention. But that very interest might prejudice the actual enquiry, if it made us think our object is to prove the truth or untruth of a future existence. It is not. We are to prove the validity or invalidity of a particular method of research in the field of faith. We are testing an instrument of the mind for verifying spiritual fact, namely, the application to belief of the question, Does it give life? This instrument or organum of research (which, if in any way a Novum Organum, is new only in the terms it adopts for the analysis of the idea of Life) we are testing over the instance of the Resurrection tenet. If the organum should fail under the trial, that would not show the tenet to be unproved, but only that it is not provable in this particular way. Our existing reasons for holding it would be left where they were. It seemed useful to insist on this caution.

I

So we set forward. Is our utterance of a belief that the Dead are raised, which is a giving of ourself, verified by a gift of Himself to us by God, so that we can know that the reciprocation which constitutes the soul's life has taken place? By what signs can we recognise that God gives this gift?

The signs can only be our own human experiences. God is known to my soul only by what He has done for my soul, and what He has done is known by the things that happen in my soul. So our question is, What things happening to me are indications that the Divine has communicated Itself to this human? In other words, what things are signs of life in the soul?

At starting we will borrow, as heretofore, the light of Nature. In the natural existence, bodily or mental, there are signs by which we recognise that vitality has been acquired by an organism. The beginning of life indeed never falls under our observation, nor is even imaginable. But the restoration of life after partial interruption can sometimes be observed. The most crucial instance we can avail ourselves of would be a man rescued from drowning, with animation suspended, and some organs functioning no longer. His rescuers apply resuscitative methods, and by manipulation of his organs of breathing produce artificial respiration, which is followed by full revival. How would they describe the fact that the man was being restored to life? They would say that now the breathing repeats itself, when they cease handling the body: the lungs go on breathing, and this persistence is a sign that the man is alive. Then they find that all the other organs are regaining life: the pulse, which had been at ebb, is now driving the tide of the blood up the emptied channels again: the skin is resuming its action; and the torpid senses are warming back into the powers of feeling, hearing, and seeing. Here is another sign of life, that the whole of the frame is coming alive together: life is not only persistent in part of the body, it is everywhere in it. Do they notice any other sign of life? Yes, they presently say the man is getting fully alive: his lungs not only breathe of themselves, but breathe deeply, his heart not only beats, but beats with strength. Until they get this sign they are not sure that the recovery is real. This is probably the kind of description which the rescuers, if not scientific but plain men, might give of the return of life. But we, for a convenience in our future argument, will take notice of a certain logic which underlies this popular language. For one sees that these physical symptoms fall naturally under three heads: the life in this body of the restored man first is continuous, then it extends throughout it, and last, it is there in force. If we give logical names to these, and say that the three signs of life in that man's organism are its extension in time, its extension in space, and its intensity of degree, we shall presently find that this scholastic refinement proves no idle pedantry, but a most useful framework or scheme to distribute and classify our thinking about the phenomena of life, as seen not in the body but the soul. The instance of life in the drowned man restored draws for us, as it were, a diagram to aid our study of how man lives unto God.

II

We turn the light then of this physical example of the phenomenon, vitality, upon the field of spiritual fact. By what signs, we ask, can we estimate the increase or the diminution of life which accompanies a belief in our soul's survival of death?

1. And first, What will be the signs we must look for in the rational nature? Let us study this in a homely fashion, and not as the scientific would; for the enquiry is one concerning our fate as men, and to prosecute it there should be need not of a philosopher, but only of a man. We shall ask then whether the life of the intelligence in a man is enhanced by his committing himself to a belief that there is a future life. Does the sign of permanence, of continuance, offer itself? Certainly it does in the mind of the race. The persistence of the expectation, in the races which it has once reached, is impressive. That impressiveness is not disturbed, but rather deepened, by the fact that

all the varying conceptions which men have formed of an After-life of the soul have successively been confessed illusions. This transiency of the form does not discredit the substance of the belief; the more it changes the more it remains the same. But what has happened in the history of the race will persuade us less than what happens in the history of ourself. Has the hope that has dawned on me of a life beyond this life held its own in time? If I find it will not let me go; that still, with all the present poverty of rational evidence and all the wealth on the other side of evidence that living creatures in nature come to an end, still the image haunts me, image frail as air and as the air invulnerable, of a world not like to this world nor all unlike it, where I and mine shall be,—then I have caught the trace of a life that beats in me and lives unto that world to which my mortal senses cannot live, but which they in vain deny. On the line of time my prophetic soul has life in its prophecy.

And then, does my whole mind join in the prophecy; do all its faculties agree in their testimony? There is a picture of the universe which my rational faculties have made for me. In that landscape of existence does this one feature, a future life, appear as an incongruous feature and out of drawing, a jarring patch in the scheme of colour : or does my consciousness own it as consistent with its other experience? Unanimity of the thoughts would be another strong indication that the mind lives in the prophecy.

Here I think we shall not refuse attention to

THE CREED OF IMMORTALITY 63

observers, who allege that the religious impulse, in which the expectation of a future is commonly a predominant element, is accompanied by a rise in the general intelligence. An argument of some value seems indicated here.

2. Then the signs of life which must be demanded in the emotional nature. For the belief in an After-life is an affection as well as an idea; and always, as the poet urges, there have been the men who 'felt within themselves the sacred *passion* of the second life.' As men can be lovers of this world, so can they also be lovers of the other world. It will have to be asked whether this affection set on things beyond not on things in the earth is an enduring affection. This can be tested in that part of the love of the world to be, the 'sacred passion', which takes concrete shape for us in a love for those others, who are of that world and will make it, if our human loves endure, what to ourself it will be. If the affection does not wane with the hours that chime for the survivor upon the clocks of mortals, the fact will not be meaningless. For in the sphere of the sensible it is so with our loves, that they suffer extinction if their object ceases to be there. The loved one become unlovable (if that can happen, as some will deny), the friend turned traitor, the child grown for ever ingrate—these are objects of love which have ceased to exist; for, though the persons may still be there, that in them which was loved is there no longer. Here are affections that have died with the death of that in the once loved one by union with

which they had their existence. We turn from these and ask, How it is with those loves of ours in which lover and beloved are now sundered by the gulf of the worlds. The relation which we name love was between these two terms, but if that other term in the love-relation is nothing any more, then love on this side the gulf must be cancelled too; God is not a God of dead men, but of living: and a lover is lover not of those who are not, but those who are. But if this love is not cancelled, if along the viewless unimaginable line, drawn and twined out of the stuff of that mystic ether of which all the web of the All is woven, there come and go vibrations that strike from heart to heart between Here and There, then the love-tie is not sundered and the loved one yet is. On the line of time my affections have life yet whole in them.

Yet again in our emotional nature there is, in the degree in which a personality is realised in us, an order and a principle, making of it a whole: our affections, like our thoughts, are a world. We shall ask therefore whether those affections which have their objects in 'the other world' belong to a world really 'other.' Whether, that is, they are incongruous and incompatible with the rest of our dispositions. Do the loves towards our parted friends move in the home of a heart as outlanders from a stranger race, or are they given a welcome and sistered there by the most gracious affections that are of the household of love? If so, then my affections have life in the measure of space.

THE CREED OF IMMORTALITY 65

3. But the Will, the faculty of action,—how is it with this? The will, as we know it most familiarly, is the will to live: it is the mainspring of that machinery by which my present existence is maintained. But my belief in an After-life is a will to live on. We ask then whether, in the determination to survive, the whole organ of volition concurs. Are we able with all our will to drink of this cup of immortality and be baptised with this baptism in the water of life? Does our personal ambition include this in its scope, and do we plan our courses of action so as to compass this achievement among the rest; or are we content to be faithful over few things, the ambitions gratifiable on earth, and not also to be rulers over the many things hereafter? If our whole will is bent on living on, that fact has significance. As was said of racers towards a rowers' goal, *Possunt quia posse videntur*, so can be said of a nobler race. If our soul be set on reaching the goal of immortality, that is no light persuasion that the goal can be attained.

But this Will, can it keep its grasp upon the belief that it will survive when hand and feet, the strong servants of the will, shall have been unmorticed from wrist and anklejoint? We men, who are maintained in temporal being by the will to live, are we conscious of a will to live on which can endure and knows no surrender? How powerfully have I seen it urged that the very old give token, as the mortal fire dies down in their bodies, of a will not to go on but to cease. Not to begin new work is their desire, but to have done with the labour of living as they are. Or have we perhaps ourselves heard some potent spirit, overworn with study or statesman cares, avow that, in the stress of the new ideas and many inventions which are changing the world, he is not sorry to be at the end of his own time? Surely here, might it be said, Nature teaches, nay, in Lucretian phrase, vociferates the truth that the organism, when its task is done, is an outworn tool to be cast upon the scrap-heap, not re-forged for other use. But I think we should interrogate Nature's meaning more closely. What will is this in the fading body that has stretched out conquered hands of surrender to death? The will to live perhaps : but not the will to live on. King Harold on the eve of Hastings fight flings himself down on his couch, refusing to task his mind with cares of battle, however urgent, any more.

"Were the great trumpet blowing doom's-day dawn,
I needs must rest"

That is not because he has no will to fight next morning. And the worn fighter, that is ourself, lays him down with even such a will, not to live, but to live on. Our death, even as some have called our birth, 'is but a sleep and a forgetting,' and is a forgetting only because it is a sleep, and because though the great trumpet *will* blow doom's-day dawn, yet this nighttime before it we needs must rest. Judge every one for himself whether or no his mortal will has a hope full of immortality.

III

We have measured life in the soul in its dimensions of time and space; have seen that it can be known whether by his belief in a future the believer's soul lives through all its parts and in all its days; have, as it were, spanned the length and breadth of the life. But besides extent and duration life must have also the dimension of intensity; we must gauge the pressure of the force within the limits of time and space. If we know the length and breadth, we have still to learn the depth and height. Otherwise, just as things inanimate, if they had but the two dimensions of surface and not the third which makes them solid, would have no real existence, so things animate do not exist as animate if their existence is only in time and space. Life, might a Pythagorean say, is a cube. Therefore, though our investigation so far of the facts which life presents to our sense-experience may have yielded us some inference for or against the survival of man, it will be an unsubstantial inference, if it ceases here. Those with whom we reason will object that 'with but little persuasion they wouldest fain persuade me to be believer in the Resurrection.' We must measure life's intensity; we must ask not only how widely and how long but also *how much* we are alive, when we hold the faith that the dead are raised.

But can this be measured? Can the methods of scientific research be applied to this? Can the intercommunion of the human spirit with the divine, which life has seemed to us, be interpreted in weights or numbers? How long that communion endures, over how great a surface of the soul the divine embrace is felt, we may somehow reckon in earthly numbers. But when it is not the spaciousness but the pressure, not the persistence but the insistence that we would know, what instrument of sense can register this? Surely one must lay down the rules and spans of men and borrow some angel's measuring-rod, such as the mystic's faculty of super-sensuous, immediate perception, which for the sake of a name he calls Intuition.

And indeed if one should press the maxim that spiritual things are spiritually discerned, it might well seem that only a mystic's method can deal with a fact so mystical as life's dimension of intensity. For this quality of forcefulness, one is led to think, will prove to be the true differentia of life, that which makes a living thing unlike all else in nature; here may be the secret we are in quest of, Life's very self.

It is not the continuance nor the spread of a life in me, accompanying the belief in another world, that works assurance of that world's reality: it is the strength of the stroke of life upon the thing that lives, and the vigour of the counterstroke from that living thing. This event that happens in my soul, that a conviction, which is unreasoned and cannot be reasoned out of me, of a Second Life for me and for mine, beats in my veins with so strenuous a pulse; that there are 'moments when I feel I cannot die' nor my own can die—this event surely can be no other than the touch of the creative Finger out of the dark that girdles my range of mortal sight. Here is what no sense reports and no science registers. Here we have done with reason, and some more ghostly function of the spirit must become our intelligencer henceforward. Why then should not that 'Intuition' of the mystic, that sense added from without to the other senses, be the organ of the soul by which we hold converse with the Beyond? This world of Nature we know by Sight: but it is Faith—not Sight—which beholds that which is invisible.

IV

The mystic, and the simple, who with his own nomenclature aims at the same mark, are right and they are wrong; right when they assert a power of human nature for which they find the name of Intuition or of Instinct, wrong when they deny the power of reason and the senses to inform of them of the unseen Reality. Their error lies here. In their conception of an organ of spiritual discernment separate in kind from the organ of sense-perception, they misconceive the world. They suppose that there are two worlds, the Seen and the Unseen, and a gulf between them which reason cannot pass. If this were so, then it might well be that there were two faculties by which to know the two, Sight and Faith, or Experience and Intuition. But then it is not so. We must change our whole way of thinking: we must make a new beginning of thought and conceive the world afresh. There is need to be born anew, to have our thoughts come again as the flesh of a little child, if we would see the kingdom of God as in earth so in heaven.

But how to make this new beginning? Some new power of our nature must deliver us from our limitations of thought. This will not be the power which we call, at least in popular speech, the reason. In our late analysis, tedious perhaps and meticulous as it may have seemed, of a believer's experience, by which we have sought to measure out the facts of vitality in the soul, we have gone as far as can be gone by the pedestrian march of logic, and it is time to let imagination lift us for a moment on a wing. We shall be exchanging the lesser teacher for the greater. Analysis, observation, induction, are true muses; but the mother of all muses is not Memory, as was fabled, but Imagination. Reason and logic are not her sisters, but her children: in the best knit argument and shrewdest analytic, it is still the Image-maker that works, though there she images, not lovely shape and scene and act, but the hard anatomy within the curves of beautiful form, the dry schedule of reason under the glowing rhyme, the naked diagram of abstract relations on which the Visions that make blest are built. This must be our teacher now if we are to learn and to keep whole and undefiled the belief that the dead shall live. For why is that belief hard? Because of the poverty of our power to image a world to come. It is not criticism, as some suppose, that breaks the resurrection hope. Criticism can do nothing to break down or to build up, until imagination has given it the

THE CREED OF IMMORTALITY 71

images which it can order and erect into a thought. If we are to reason out to ourselves a faith in a world in which we are to live on, first we must image forth that world. That is what is hard. For it must be a world where time (as we tell ourselves, perhaps too hastily) cannot be, and where space will have no meaning: but how image anything without this frame of time and space! The troubles of Time overcome our mind. To think of an end may choke our spirit, but to think of an endlessness—this too is a fear that hath some torment. From that gulf of an infinite, homeless sky, we are half fain to take shelter in the tent which some philosophers erect for us, when they say, in our day as in Paul's, that the resurrection is passed already, for behold we have risen in a New Life of character achieved on this homelike floor of present earth, and need not to look on to that vasty hall of Futurity. Or the troubles of Space go over us. With what body do they come, the dead? With what body indeed, when we ask it, came from His empty tomb the Risen Lord? And how shall I bear up against the leaden weight of Nature's monotonous affirmation that all the children of space came from earth, and to earth all return and none of them are found any more again? Almost our spirit is tempted to seek relief in that Eastern creed, that as the body crumbles back into nameless dust, so will the soul re-melt, as cloud into sky, as wave into ocean, and be lost in the unfeatured Whole, which at once is the All and is the Nothingness.

From this prison of logic the liberator must be the

Imagination, which again and again has liberated the human spirit. As when she was the angel of the Lord who took the Syrian shepherd by the hand and led him forth at night to look upon the stars and know the number of his seed, and the Oneness of the God, who was Father of all the family in heaven and earth. Or as when she was guide to that sage of Greece, master of Roman Lucretius, who 'first of mortals dared to lift eyes against a tyrant faith, Religion, the Binder of souls, brow-beating mortals with her scowl from a lowering heaven.' And is not our prison of thought very like to that from which Lucretius would lead out his countrymen. For they imaged the place of man's destiny as a narrow floor of earth-dust overarched by a low dome of iron firmament, 'studded with burning stars.' From this close place he would have them come forth with him and his master. They must venture out beyond 'the flaming walls of the universe' and watch the tides of creative energy 'bearing all things through a void'; for so they would learn the width and wonder of the All, and the idle terrors would be withered off their souls. And are not we lodged, we too, in such a prison-world, with even such narrowing and stifling walls, and even such a gaoler of it to brow-beat us with idle fears, when we conceive of a human existence in that image and likeness which our sense-experience has constructed for us; and which we suppose, by 'a weak disabling of ourselves,' is the only image which that experience is competent to build. The world, which alone we think is known to us through our senses, is a closed circle or hollow sphere of matter, of which floor and wall and roof are just so far and no further from us than the furthest points to which on all sides our mortal senses reach. This sphere of the temporal and actual encloses as in a dome the soul of man : she sits at centre of it, and the senses are the radii with which she spans the circumference, the arms which she can stretch to feel the bounds of her strait prison, the world that now is. Doubtless she knows, or at least hopes, that this world is not all her being's world. Above that near, hard firmament of the vault of space, this low-browed crypt of mortal time, there is another world, the Eternal: she prays some day to inherit it. But meanwhile this Eternal is to her another world : that is her error and her sorrow. It is another : the worlds she knows of are two; they are not one. And the powers by which she knows them are two; they are not one. There are the senses, with the reason to unify them, by which to know the present world; there is some other organ by which to know the world to come. It must be faith, says the soul to herself, if she is simple Christian : it must be Intuition, she says, if she is also philosopher. That is her error; and the pity of it is much.

V

For all the while she has an instrument of knowledge by which she can know the things outside the range within which her senses seem tethered. That instrument is and is not Intuition, and it is not and is

Experience. The organ by which the soul knows the eternal world is Herself. It is her total nature, the whole personal being which has the name of man.

What is this Self, and of what is it made? It is built up of the manifold relations in which the personal being, a man, stands to the whole of Being. Such relations are seeing, hearing, touching; and such are understanding, feeling, and putting force upon things. This organ, the whole Self, has its functioning, as all the lesser organs have, in fulfilling and maintaining these relations to the Whole: it sees and touches with eye and hand, and with mind or heart it perceives or is emotionally affected. One of these energies is that which we call Knowing. But it is only one of them: it is the sensitiveness of only a portion of that total surface of sensibility which the Self exposes to contact with the world outside it, and by which it lives, moves, and has its being in that world. In the activity called Knowing, the soul, as it were, specialises: her generalised function of relating herself to or living unto the world becomes a specific function, that which we call Thought. But this faculty of Thought or Knowing differs from the faculty of Being or Living only as a species differs from its genus. Thinking is the species of which Being is the genus. When, therefore, the soul, instead of merely relating herself generally to the world, enters into the particular relation of knowing it, she does not cross a frontier from one kind of action to another; she only makes her relations with Reality more definite, complex, and intimate. But before she 'knew' Reality in the common sense of knowing, she was alive to it: the relations in which she stood to it were already there: she felt the reality, she re-acted towards it. To be in these relations to the world of fact was already to know the world: not to know it well, but to know. This is the meaning with which we assert that the soul has an organ by which she knows the Eternal Facts. That organ is Herself: by living unto the Eternal with all her self, touching and touched by it, she knows it.* And when she is aware of being alive unto this fact among eternal facts,—a world to come of which she is part and parcel, a law of survival of men that die,—then she has learned that she is immortal, and her belief in the Resurrection of the dead is a right belief.

VI

It was imagination, we said, that must give us this vision of the world and of the faculty by which we know it. But it must give it us by an image. So one images to oneself the life of some deep-sea creature which lives and moves and has its being in boundless ocean. Round it floats an enveloping sphere of sea-water: this is the near environment to which its

---

*To speak of a Self which at once knows and does not know the remoter world will appear to be an intrusion on ground over which new philosophies of the Subconscious are working. This territory, however, lies for these philosophies within their 'sphere of influence' (in the statesman's phrase) but not of occupation; and beside their metaphor of the Subliminal Consciousness there is room for others such as our own, attempting the interpretation of the problem.

organism makes the response which is of immediate necessity for its existence. But that sphere of water is continuous with all the water of ocean from pole to pole; and to all that world of water this living creature is, as it were, alive, is in vital continuity with it. Into that little envelope of fluid the earthquake a thousand miles away sends a tremor from its spasm; into it steals the warm touch of a far-off gulf-stream, the cold of arctic ice-mountains, the freshness from the rain-floods poured off a thousand hills, the saltness from the briny heart of ocean which no rivers of the sweet rains can reach; hither the arrows of the sunlight pierce with spent, pointless shafts, through the unsounded dark, and the roar of battling navies descends with a smothered rumour into the deaf abyss. All the liquid world affects its creature with its warmths and rigours, sweetnesses or salt, its lights and echoes, its pressures and its thrills.

This is our parable and thus we would interpret it. A human soul moves in a near environment of the things the man hears, sees, touches, the world of time and space. By his relations to these he has his life of the present. But not all his life. He is also living to other facts than the facts near him. Things that happen further off, the things of what we call the Eternal Order, these send their vibrations to and through the envelope of his mortal conditions, and these too deliver their stroke upon his being. We do not say that he 'knows' them; for we do not say he sees, hears, handles them, since we cannot assign to

THE CREED OF IMMORTALITY 77

any one sense the thing that happens to him, when the impact of a remote happening falls upon him. Yet he does know them by the Self which is spread through all his senses. He knows them by what happens to that self, by a response which the self makes to the stimulation, though the stimulus is not recognised and named. If the effect of that stimulus on the organism of a soul has been an enhancement of that soul's vitality, then in this way the soul knows the force which causes it. The creature of our sea-parable knows of the solar beam that travels all but extinguished into its dark ring of water, not because it has knowledge of a sun in the sky which visits it, but because an animation quickens in it by the touch, and because thus that far, unseen sun is a fountain of life to it: in its light it sees light. So the man knows the day of his visitation from the world beyond sense, not because he has descried in heaven a day-spring from on high, which has visited him in his mortal dark, but because his nature has been thrilled and strung, lightened and quickened, eased and comforted, by an impact he cannot name nor even clearly discriminate among his sensations, but which has wrought these effects upon him. With that Power unseen is the well of life, and in its light he has seen light.

VII

Yet in a measure he can name, not the force itself, but his experience of it. For that experience (this we want here to assert and later make good) is a thing that happens to the man not in the spirit only but also in the body. For the body, or flesh, is the soul so far as related to this world, the time and space world. This human frame of sense, and of mind and character embodied in sense, this manifestation of a spirit in matter, is in response to the supernal reality, it is acted on by it and re-acts; it is visited and knows the day of its visitation. Things happen to that human frame, the flesh of a spirit: thoughts happen on the brain, emotions happen in the heart, actions are performed by the hand; and all these are effects in the flesh of an influence from the spiritual world. These happenings can be noted, verified, and in a degree estimated, can be known in fact even as all else is known that is knowable. Yes, in some sort flesh and blood do reveal to us the act upon us of the Father who is in heaven. In homelier language, there can be some science even of Faith.

VIII

The Lord our God is one God, and God's world is one world, and the knowledge by which we know it is one. That is our contention. God's will is done as in heaven so in earth; and God's way is known as by heaven, so by earth; not by spirit only but also by flesh. The mystery of divine vitality doth already work in the children of obedience, while they are yet in the body, and we can have our mortal senses exercised to discern good and evil, as good and evil are in the world of eternal fact.

But our research is into truth more particular than the existence of an eternal order. Concerning this momentous particular in that order, the Resurrection of the Dead, and how man can know it, we have chosen to be called in question. It will have to be asked presently, what cannot be asked now, whether this great article of the creed is a truth which can be verified only by the tests which in all times and places all believers have been wont to employ—the tests of Scriptural authority, church tradition, deductive reasoning, and mystical intuition, which is a Christian's second sight. It will be asked whether human nature has not, in its present low estate of mortal existence, a knowledge of this particular fact of eternal existence, —that man whose life is unto time and space also has life unto the timeless and spaceless reality, and because It lives he shall live also. And it will be asked whether that knowledge is not like all his other knowledge, and attainable in part by use of these same natural senses, which light up for him that little arc of the whole circle of Being, a man's time on earth.

To ask these questions is to put on trial a proposed method of spiritual research. It is to endeavour to make good the assertion just now ventured, that the soul has an organ of proof by which she is informed of eternal fact, and that this organ is Herself. Its functioning is all that activity by which the soul lives to the seen and actual world, but also to the unseen and yet more real world. In part, and not in little part, this activity is exercised through the use of the natural senses by which all other experience is harvested. We do not put aside the well-recognised verifying instruments of Tradition or Reasoning, nor do we deny the alleged faculty of Intuition. We do claim that Traditionalist and Intuitionalist should not reject this instrument of Sense-perception, and give to their own instruments work which the bare senses can achieve. It is true that we walk by faith and not by sight. Yet, for some of the near reaches of our pilgrim road, Faith, even she, is also Sight.

IV

THE CREED OF THE RESURRECTION

[March 19th, 1911.]

"He that wonders shall reign"
"Wonder at that which is before you."

Traditional sayings of Christ
preserved by Clement of Alexandria
(*Strom.* II 9, 45)

IV

THE CREED OF THE RESURRECTION

PSALM CXXVI. 1-5.—"When the Lord turned again the captivity of Sion, then were we like unto them that dream. Then was our mouth filled with laughter and our tongue with joy. Then said they among the heathen, The Lord hath done great things for them. Yea, the Lord hath done great things for us already, whereof we rejoice. Turn our captivity, O Lord, as the rivers in the south"

I

WE have now ventured to name an organ of knowledge by which the soul knows the world it lives in. It is an instrument which must not be identified either with the Senses, by which alone many think we experience fact; or with that Intuition by which a few conceive that we can apprehend remoter Being. The organ by which we know the facts that lie beyond the range of the senses is, we ventured to say, our Self. This Self lives to the world, the whole world, material and spiritual: and it is by living to this world that it knows it. The measure of its knowledge is the measure of the life by which the Self responds to That which Is.

This position, that to be alive to God's world is to know that world, was attained by exercise of that faculty of the Reason which we call Imagination. By it we have pictured the world as a sphere of Being, one and continuous throughout, not really divided into provinces of Seen and Unseen, with a blind wall between them at which the march of reason must halt. All motions that take place anywhere within this sphere of the All must move through it everywhere, just as, in a similitude which we framed, the sea-creature in ocean's depth receives upon its body some impulse, however dulled, from every agitation in the remotest parts of its liquid continuous world of waters. Therefore the soul, while conscious mainly of such agitations as occur in its near envelopment of the bodily existence, must also receive the impact, with however infinitesimal an effect, of the events or facts which originate in the further environment called the spiritual existence. To that impact it must respond, as really, though not as consciously, as it responds in its physical organism to the stimulus of the external forces of nature, the touch of air and water, of storm and sunshine, of hurtful shocks which must be shunned. That is to say, the soul of a man is a personal being which extends, potentially at least, and to a degree actually, through all the world. Each soul, one must venture it, is in all Being and knows it all, by making that response to it which is to live unto its world. As on a lake the water-ring about a thrown pebble spreads ideally to the shore everywhere, and a myriad other such rings would over-run it and reach the same margin, and each become one with the whole lake-circle, yet each remain itself, not lost in the whole nor the whole in it,—so is it with the universe and the souls of men. Our soul can grow till it gather into its circumference all the world, and every soul can do the same, and they cannot be numbered and yet none is lost.

But there is an image which will suit our purpose better. The soul is a web of far-spreading threads which are so many sensitive nerves, with its centre, the Ego or Self, placed (if it have a centre, as is not certain) on the plane of earth. It stretches the network of perceptive nerves out and out, till they cross the earth-horizon and travel on, unsevered and alive and sentient still, into the infinite, where abide the great Facts which are the works of God, the Facts by response to which He who made us ordained our souls to live. When our soul does respond to the touch of these Facts, it lives to them. And when it lives to them, then and thus it knows them. When it lives. That living to the Facts of the Eternal World must be a living of all the soul, not of a part. Not of the mind which lives to facts by a reasoning, but also of the heart which lives by a feeling towards them, and of the will which lives by an act that meets their action. The soul of the wise man, said the Greek, is spectator of all time and all existence. That would be a too sparing saying of the soul. She is not spectator only of creation: she is also lover of it and actor with it. Not by Vision does she know the world what it is; she knows it by a Vision, by an Affection, by a Deed. *Visio Dei Vita Hominis.*

II

From Imagination's watchtower, which we climbed to overlook the world, we would now descend and regain the path our quest was pursuing. We had left it at this point. It was necessary for our argument that we should particularise the experiences in the organism of a soul, which would be signs that it was receiving life from that unseen reality to which it had given itself by the act of belief. This life, we thought, was to be measured in the three dimensions of Permanence or Extension in Time, Pervasiveness or Extension in Space, and Intensity or Force. This third, however, seemed to be a dimension which can *not* be measured. We hazarded that this was because Intensity is the very secret of life, is Life Itself. But there we paused, and betook ourselves to the vantage height from which we hoped to see the wider field, by relation to which this portion of the field would be more intelligible. It is as we hoped.

For now, when we come to ask how we can discern the intensity of life in the soul, when by the act of belief it delivers itself over to the believed reality—a friend's survival after death,—we find it is possible to discern that sign of life; and possible because we learn that the world is one world, and the spirit of man dwells always in the whole world, and not, as we were fancying, first in the one province and afterwards in the other.

Among the facts of the eternal world is this fact,

THE CREED OF THE RESURRECTION 87

our faith says,—the friend who has departed this present life. If that fact, his personal being, is there, then the fact must have an action upon our personal being; for our personality is also within that world. What then is that action?

It is the stroke of a conviction which falls upon my soul. I know in myself that it is so. He is there. I know it, not because that conviction abides and will not away, not because it fills all the chambers of my mind and heart : but because my conviction is so strong. I cannot keep it out : it is the violent who takes by force the kingdom of my Self. I am sure of this Real Thing, my friend alive, because the life in my soul that kindles on that belief not only endures, not only pervades me, but also beats with such a mighty pulse.

'No' says the truster in positive science. 'The mourner doubtless has sometimes that conviction you name. But it is an illusion. It is memory of the past that still lights up the present; it is the trail of a meteor, luminous for a while; it is the shining arc in the wake of the brandished torch; it is the dreamed touch of a hand that has vanished, the sound in fancy's echo of a voice that now is still.'

We will see whether this is so.

The mystic, on the other hand, says 'Yes. There is in you a sense beside your senses. These cannot know the world beyond, but this Intuition can know it.'

We will see whether it is so, or whether it is even better than so.

For we are daring to think that it is both as you, brother, suppose, that we have a sense of eternal reality beside our senses of mortal man, and also, as you have foregone to think, that these same mortal senses can tell us something of the great News; and that beautiful on the mountains even of our low earth, the Flesh, are the feet of messengers who bring us good tidings of this good.

III

For to us it seems that this knowledge of things in the world beyond the horizons of sense, which you call intuitional knowledge, and another critic calls no knowledge but illusion, is the same knowledge,—not indeed throughout, but for a great reach of its extent, —the same knowledge as that whereby we know the facts of which positive science informs us;—such a fact, for example, as this, that some now present living man, any friend of mine, exists and has to do with me.

For how do I know that what stands there is my friend, and not an illusion of the vision, a phantasm? I know him in a threefold way, by my thought of him, my feeling for him, my action towards him. For my mind has an experience of him as a person, so has my affectional nature, so has my active. But I know him, be it observed, not by *my* thought, *my* love, *my* will, but by *our* thoughts, loves, wills. I know the person of a friend, the thing that he is in truth, by his thoughts and mine that interchange, our affections

THE CREED OF THE RESURRECTION 89

that interlock, our purposes that interact. If when my thought went out to him, no thought of his came back to me; when my love expanded towards him, no love on his part came out towards me; when my will moved to act on him, no will in him either received me or repelled me or went any whither along with mine:—if no relation between him and me came into being, either of friendship, or (to make our reasoning complete) of hostility or rejection either—then there was no such thing before me as I had for a moment believed to be my friend in the body: there was an illusion of the eye, a phantom, or, if any object, something that was not a person.

All this knowledge, then, of another person who is with myself in the sphere of things temporal is a knowledge of the relations which exist between him and me. This is a mere commonplace of philosophy. And all these relations between us are experiences of the senses; they are seen, felt, heard by me through the organs in me which deal with the facts of the world that now is. They are matters verifiable by science, though, in the case of the perceptions of personal relations, not an exact science; while yet it is a science which satisfies the enquirer's self, if no one else. My sense-experience convinces me that the friend is there and is a person of such or such a nature; and if some thorough-going sceptic warns me that I cannot prove anything exists except my own personality, I am not impressed. On the contrary, I find myself in agreement with the commonsense philosopher, at whose simpleness it is usual to smile, who confutes the idealist by the pressure of hand or foot, which he says demonstrates the existence of matter. I see that he is wise. For he has proved the reality of substance by its reaction to his touch, made known to him in sensations of a limb which dealt it; and I prove my friend's reality in the same way. I act towards him, and there is a reaction from his personality upon my own : I know it by the strokes of a force which fall upon my sentient self.

IV

This is how we convince ourselves that our friend exists in the world of matter. Our conviction, when we have it, that a friend who has left the material world still exists in the spiritual, is a conviction of the same quality. We discover that between us and him there are relations. This is what we come to when we analyse the insistent consciousness, which at first seems an inscrutable instinct, that a friend is not dead, but alive. It is a discovery that our soul is in response to him, and his to ours; things pass between us. Thus, first on the side of its intelligence, our soul is in this response; there is an intercourse of mind and mind. For this we will not cite the evidence of those articulate messages from the unseen world, 'airy tongues that syllable men's names,' which some living men and women have believed themselves to receive. Such evidence appeals to the recipients, less to others. And again, if we glance at the labours of some who are now seeking by methods of strict science to verify communications between the living and the 'discarnate,' it is that we may bid them a brotherly God-speed in a quest so lawfully and reverently pursued by them, and in a spirit so wholly noble, while we may not call in aid of our own research results of an enquiry, which is still only on its way. We shall ask instead, What think ye of this fact which we find in ourselves,—this assurance which fastens on our consciousness and will not away from it, that the friend who died is not dead, but survives? This assurance is a fact, whatever be its explanation. It is a thing among things, whatever be the law of things which it exhibits. There really are for man 'the moments when he feels he cannot die' and that his brother has not died. *Cogito, ergo sum,* avowed the metaphysician: 'I think, therefore I am.' *Cogito ergo est,* 'I think, and therefore my friend is,' the plain man may pronounce as a reason for the faith that is in him. His conviction is inarticulate, formless, abstract: there is no message in it from the further world, 'telling what it is to die': it is not in word, it is only in power. But in power it is: it possesses, it masters the mind: we try to shake off its domination, and let the other image of an existence ended, a life consumed in the fires of Not-Being, sit in its place upon the throne of our intelligence. But the image of a life that lives on will not yield its place, and the other vision is a strengthless phantom that goes browbeaten away. Of this fact of human experience an account must be rendered. There is the account which many enquirers render: the image of a continued life is subjective, they say, it is a fume of the mind, a memory mistaken for a present experience; it is the fancied sensation in a limb which the surgeon's knife has severed. We claim that our account of it fits the phenomenon more closely: this is the vibration, we say, from a distant consciousness which beats upon our own. It is known already that mind can send such vibrations upon another mind across wide distances on the earth-plain: why should the telepathy fail when the space to be traversed lies in part along the earth-plain and in part along reaches of the wider world? Why, in the communication of spirits, should the line break at the horizon of matter; seeing that matter has no horizon line in fact, but world of matter flows into world of spirit, as sea melts into sea, and in the one continuous ether of which all the worlds are built there rises no disconnecting barrier to stay the current of the travelling force, which is a thought?

V

Thought, do I say? Do we know the friend is there in the Unseen only because we *think* his survival? That survival is made known to us not only by a relation to him which we experience in our rational soul, but also by what happens in our affections. 'Peace, let it be, for I loved him, and love him for ever; the dead are not dead but alive.' So cries a mourner in a poet's verse, and those also who cannot verse their love, can avow it. The love for the lost comrade is there: what shall be assigned as its origin? If illusion or memory's trick is the interpretation offered, the lover who is mourner will answer that you have not spelt his case; he knows what love living and experienced is, and he knows what love dead and remembered is; it is not memory, but experience, that is with him now. This too he knows, that this love has joy for him. But were the love unreal, were it a passion that found no response, were it a yearning for that which is no more nor ever can be again, the love would be to him not a joy but a bitterness, a tragic pain, like the memory of an affection for a yet living friend who has proved unworthy of being loved, a memory which we would drive away from our brain and breast. Or again, the impulse thus denied an outlet would be the ache of a faculty denied its exercise, the woe of the strong, wild creature caged. But this love, though it may kindle tears, has not suffering for him, but joy and enlargement, it has the blessing of peace, a savour not of death, but of life unto life. So then that assurance of a friend's existence is not a conviction of the mind alone, but also a passion of the heart. And the passion is there in power. It does not only persist, it does not only pervade our being: the rhythm of life which pulses in the heart-beat of this love is also strong. It is in the length and in the breadth, but also in the depth.

VI

And yet there is a third element in the assurance we are analysing. The soul is thinker and lover, but also it is actor. Towards the parted friend it can have also a will.

When the idea is raised of an intercourse between two wills, one in the temporal, the other in the suprasensuous sphere, a broad field of the human consciousness is stirred by that challenge. Men have always and everywhere held, in a surmise or even a conviction, the belief in such intercourse, whether for succour or antagonism. St. Paul wrestles not against flesh and blood, but unseen evil wills; Joan of France fights not till she has conferred with her ghostly 'Council' among the trees; soldiers in old Greece and soldiers in new Japan have thanked the spirits of the past for championship in the battle of to-day; Harold of England tells his men before a victory

> "Last night King Edward came to me in dreams;
> He told me we should conquer,"

and the world has tales enough of revisitant forms dimly glimpsed in postures of aid over child or friend in danger. These things we have called pious fancies. What do we say of the experience, known inwardly, though rarely and in secrecy professed, of not a few from the days of Socrates to our own,—the experience of a monition or an impulsion to act or refrain from acting? 'It came on me,' one says, 'to do this or

THE CREED OF THE RESURRECTION 95

that : I could not see why, but I did it, and then I saw, for it was the thing that needed to be done.' What do we say of this touch of spur or bridle? 'Mere coincidence' perhaps you call it. Some of us, then, will prefer to err with Socrates, who named it a 'Something Spiritual.' And, while one muses on these things, it breaks upon one that just now certain new readings of natural fact are pointing a finger towards this old reading of facts transcending nature. That will can sometimes act on distant will across terrestrial intervals is a truth which, to state the position modestly, can now hardly be refused the name of a scientific verity; and it needs a somewhat self-confident scepticism to scout the hopes of Research that she may bridge the intervals which lie for part of the distance within the Unseen. But while Research is still groping her way across, some of us 'believing where we cannot prove,' will ride out on private adventure. We shall come back avowing that there went Another on our quest : a presence in the dark barred a false path against us; a tender hand drew us aside to a generosity, a forgiveness, a loving-kindness; our nerve was steeled for a peril by a touch of steel, that was the temper of some fighter of the past, so that

> "Almost I felt him fold
> An arm in mine to fix me to the place
> That way he used ;"

or in a lonely wrestle of the reason we were not alone, there was again a dialectic of two souls, and ours sought a truth with his.

So then along the line of this third strand of consciousness, the will by which man acts, along this also as well as the strands of thought and emotion, the communion passes of the Seen and the Unseen. Threefold is the knowledge that has come. It is a conviction, and it is a passion, and it is a power. How strong is the fibre of this bond which knits us to the Unseen! The doubts which interpret our experience by the theory of Illusion might make the bond perish, could they strain its members one by one. A threefold cord is not so quickly broken. The man who feels the life quicken in brain and heart and will at once, must be alive indeed unto some reality. By an organ of knowledge which is his Self, and by a function of it which is the sense of living, this man knows of a fact beyond the veil of bodily sense. That reality among the realities is this Other, whom here he loved and lost. In that death they are not divided. They hold sweet counsel yet together, and still in the great house of God they walk as friends.

VII

Let us briefly sum this reasoning up. We have reasoned that where we speak of 'knowing' an eternal truth we misname that energy of the soul: we are using the name of a part for a name of the whole. The soul knows a truth not by the workings of its intelligence, but by the energy of its whole being. This energy is the movement by which the soul approaches and touches the unseen reality which it

THE CREED OF THE RESURRECTION 97

seeks to know. In that contact the soul finds life. There happens a communion of the mortal self and a Self in the eternal world : by that interchange each lives unto each. That sense of life received by the soul is its evidence of things not seen. Hereby it knows the Resurrection of the Dead.

Yet we are not of those reasoners who by retreating with their argument into the shadowland of myth, evade refutation. On the contrary, it is our main contention that this evidence of things not seen is rendered in things that do appear. This life of the soul which results from its contact with a reality beyond the range of the senses, is a sensible fact. Our senses receive upon them the stroke of the reality which has met us, and they register that force so that we can read it off, as we read off by our instruments the weight of winds, volume of rains, the heat of the sunbeam. The signs which register our contact with this reality—the survival of man—are the conviction which grips the mind, the passion which strains the heart, the energy which animates the will. These phenomena are sensible phenomena. They have even their material equivalents, which could be read, had science the insight, in the thrills of the brain and the labour of the blood. This eternal blazon can, in some measure, be to ears of flesh and blood. But at least for the science, less exact but still science, of psychology, the soul offers itself to observation : it can be observed whether the intelligence has or has not an assurance, and the will a purpose, which are vivid.

This observation of what happens to a man's soul in the flesh is in some measure possible even for another than the man's self : so far as we can estimate character in another, so far can we observe these psychic changes in his inward nature, which we claim as effects of a cause which lies in the super-sensuous region. Doubtless that is not very far. But our argument that the proof of spiritual fact is discernible in fleshly fact, is not thereby invalidated. For as the heart knoweth its own bitterness and a stranger doth not intermeddle with its joy, yet none the less the joy or the bitterness is to the heart certain, and assures it that there is a real cause of what it feels, even so is it here. To whom if not to my own soul is it necessary that proof of the eternal life be given? When I have found it, how gladly will I share it with others. But first, it is myself who crave assurance. I shall not find it by a stranger's eyes : he cannot appease the bitterness of my doubt, no, nor intermeddle with my joy when in my house of life unto me is born my faith.

VIII

Here then is our reasoning. It has been made possible, let me recall, only where the way has been made plain for the discourse of reason by a more primal faculty, the imagination. The human soul, an heir of the wide universe, is by its earthly generation born into the narrow dwelling-house, her nursery after birth, which we name Experience, meaning the experience of the senses. 'Thence she comes forth to re-behold the stars,' the stars of all the heaven, and to learn that in this All she is at home. There she can know even as she is known, by a knowledge which is the life that builds the world and binds it into one.

That the knowledge of the eternal world comes not but by imagination is no new doctrine, but a very old. The Greek who said in his pragmatic way that philosophy begins in wonder, was wording this truth, though in part only, for wonder is more than the curiosity which leads to science. Far nearer came his brother Greek who praised that myth which made Thaumas, Spirit of Wonder, to be parent of Iris, winged messenger of heaven, the Spirit of divine-human communion. And nearer still comes our re-wording of the truth, when we speak of imagination in her activity of Wonder. For Imagination wondering—what is it? It is not surprise, with which we tend to confound it; for surprise is only the attempt to adjust the self to an emergency; to be surprised is to be aware that something new comes over us, a peril or an opportunity. The least conscious of living things, the dull beast, the fish, the insect, is susceptible of surprise. Wonder is the reaction not to the new simply, but to the new which is also the great. It is the reaction of the self to the contact with greatness, whether the greatness of the vast, or the strong, or the beautiful. It is a poet's Adam, gazing for the first time on the starry world revealed by night-fall, when

"Hesperus with the host of heaven came,
And lo! creation widened in man's view."

Wonder is that vital act by which the soul attempts to relate itself to the world, as discovered to be great beyond her knowledge of it; and this act, like all acts that are vital, is an uprender of herself to this greatness which renders itself to her. We know the eternal world by that effort of our spirit to live unto that world, which we have called imaginative wonder. In that effort there is hardihood at once and awe, as the soul peers out from the shell of her temporal encompassment, ventures to confront the greatness which is for her, and the heart fears and is enlarged. 'He that wonders shall reign' is a word recorded by a too doubtful tradition as a saying of Jesus. It is a true saying, even if of less authority. He shall be inheritor of the Kingdom of Life who dares lift up his eyes to heaven and wonder at the vastness of his doom.

IX

If, then, our faculty of sense-perception gives us intelligence of facts in the spiritual region, what do we say of the faculty, which some claim for the soul, of knowing supra-mundane fact intuitively? We shall offer the surmise that this Intuition is a name for the soul's capacity of experiencing fact by that part of its organism which extends, according to the metaphor, beyond the circle of the temporal order into the eternal order. Those outstretched threads of the web, as we figured it, of sentient being, perceive by touch the forces which move in that more rarified atmosphere, and they make those adjustments of the self to the far environment which, if they prosper, are acts of life. But these members of our total consciousness, since they lie in the supra-sensuous region, cannot record their experiences of the facts they encounter there in terms of the temporal order, cannot translate into the language of sight and sound that which eye háth not seen nor ear hath heard, but which it yet does somehow enter into the heart of man to conceive by a faculty of personality to which, since we need to name it, let us give the name Intuition.

Sense experience, soul intuition, these, then, are not two kinds of knowing, but successive stages of one knowledge. Here in our mortal estate, our cognisance of the immortal reality, and of those lives in it which for each of us breathing men are our own dearest concern in that reality,—this cognisance must mainly be that experience of the senses; though doubtless it is for ever over-passing the ideal but not actual horizon line of space and time. The hungerer after communion with souls now on that line's further side is like that tender singer of exiled and rescued Israel to whom had been vouchsafed, in the remnant restored, a pledge of his people's full return, while the fulfilment tarried yet. 'When the Lord turned again the captivity of Zion, then were we like unto them that dream.'

And when the Lord turns again for ourselves to-day our captives of Zion; turns them again, restores, by that frail communion in which through the experience of one organ of the soul, our mortal sense, life touches parted life again, then we, too, are like unto them that dream. The Lord hath done great things for us already, even this scant restoring to us of severed souls, whereof we rejoice. Yet 'turn our captivity, O Lord, like the rivers in the south,' when the sweet rains have filled the desolate hollows of their bed. Turn again to each yearning spirit of man the captives of mortality, in that river that brims its bank, of a communion where all of their soul shall commune with all of ours.

X

To what are we being led by our study of the belief in the Life Everlasting? We have reached a goal, to find it a starting-point. For in learning how we of this day believe in the survival of our brother who has died, we perhaps have been learning how men in the first days believed that Christ, who for us men and for our salvation died on the cross, rose again on the third day from the dead. Are we this way finding a clue to the problem of the Resurrection of Jesus?

The difficulties which beset our understanding of the Appearances of Jesus after the Passion are largely the perplexities which arise from the mingling in the story of two orders of fact, the bodily and the spiritual, supposed to be not only distinct, but disparate and incompatible. We need but name the empty tomb, the vacant grave-clothes, the body offering itself to touch, yet more unsubstantial than the air, the scars of wounds showing on limbs which were now of spirit

THE CREED OF THE RESURRECTION 103

texture not of the human clay. The hypotheses applied hitherto to these contradictions have failed. The notion, held by simple men, of a human organism dead but reanimated, is a childish thing, helpless to explain the matter. The counter theory of Visions, meaning self-illusions of the mind of witnesses, is no less helpless to explain the fact of the Christian life generated in the vision-seers, and through them in the Christian community. The interpretation that the risen body was a 'spiritual' body is no more than a reverent name for our ignorance. But by the hypothesis, which in our present train of reflections has presented itself, there seems to open a direction more hopeful for the solving of the enigma.

For in that hypothesis the spiritual and the material are not disparates, but intercommunicables: the world is one, and the soul's knowledge of it is one.

We apply it here, and ask whether that which happened to the Disciples who saw the Lord Jesus risen, was not the same thing as what happens when one of ourselves attains the belief, that his own dead friend is not dead but alive.

That happening, as we sought to analyse it, was that some impulsion falls upon our conscious being from a reality in the eternal world. The stroke is received alike upon the spiritual sensibility of our organism and upon the physical. Our body and soul alike make the response of a vital intercommunion with the unseen reality, which is the act of knowing that reality.

But this action, call it a knowing or a living, is an

action of the whole man together. It is realised in the senses as well as in the spirit, and the motions of mind, affections, will are reactions in the flesh which register the vibrations reaching them from the world beyond sense.

XI

That analysis we laboured enough : this application of it we will not labour. We will try to render it after the method of the great master among Greeks of the art of presenting spiritual truth, who when dialectic and logic had done their best upon a problem, would seek the last interpretation of it in the imaginative expedient of 'truth embodied in a tale' or in the parable of a fancy. Our imagining, however, of how men became witness to the Resurrection shall be no mythos, as Plato used, but a tale of a human experience; only a tale retold, not as it has been chronicled with so slender particularity, but as a human sympathy can fill in that bare outline with significances that may be for other time and place.

And, as at our outset we tried to reconstruct the act of belief in a Peter, so let us here attempt the faith-story of a John.

And be it premised that any student of the Christ-fact who may doubt whether that faith-story, as told in the Fourth Gospel, is history otherwise than as ideas are history, may yet be able to listen to our reconstruction, though translating it perhaps the while into terms of his own theory.

What is it that holds fast in a spell the young man who has come out from the dark of the garden tomb and hangs tranced beside the dusk doorway, like unto them that dream? It is Wonder, the parent of Communion, that holds him tranced. 'Here we laid fore-yesterday,' he muses, 'the Master's body, dead. And here lie to-day the dead man's robes, but not he. Where then? What is this that is happening to us?... That saying of his 'On the third day I shall rise.'... He said it... can this thing be that?' And here there is convulsion in the mind of John. All that familiar scene, the world he knew, is shaken as by earthquake and flung backward into the perspectives of immensity. The walls of space roll apart, and gasping he looks out into the infinite. The Lord is in this place, and he knew it not.... The house of God.... The gate of heaven. With lips parted and a soul that opens to receive the flood of a mystery that is being given him, he casts himself in whole surrender upon God, whose ways are in the deep but His footsteps are not known. It is the beloved disciple's moment of Wonder. He is flinging away his conception hitherto of the world of fact, by which a man entombed is a man who exists no longer, and he is drinking in, as it were, through amazement's opened lips, this new conception, vast but as yet unfeatured, of a world where things are not so, but where a man, it seems, can fall on sleep and yet not see corruption. John saw and believed. He that wonders shall reign: and this is the wondering of John.

Wonder must have her perfect work. How is it with John now at nightfall, sitting back in the shadows of the Upper Room; groups of the brethren near him, restless men, faces haggard with surmise and doubt, glances of one at other that answer question with question? A knock, and unbolting. Peter enters, a smothered fire in his eyes, a message that is stifled on his lips: 'I saw Him.' Silence then, except for the heartbeats loud in each one's ear. Again a knock. Two wan, dazed faces in the doorway, framed by the dark. 'He was with us but now...we knew Him when He brake the bread...then He was gone... but it was He.' Silence once more, and hearts beating louder in the ear. Heartbeats; and a mightier Something than the beat of heart, pulsing upon the soul of each. Something that draws near and near. Something with a footfall that enters the house of life of each disciple, that echoes clearer, like strokes of a bell increasing on the ear, as it comes inward from soul's outer gate to inner chamber: divine Reality coming home to men. Coming home, ah! even to their fleshly senses; a Presence that lays its touch even on the organs by which man sees and hears, till these also stir and quicken, and an energy goes forth of them to meet the creative energy of God shed abroad in heart of man, and to know the Christ because unto the Christ their soul in all its senses lives.

Then—then—who spoke? Is it John, that way he has? Is it speech at all? Ah, surely that disciple whom Jesus loved says 'Brothers, it is the Lord.'

THE CREED OF THE RESURRECTION 107

And the Lord is there indeed. In His habit as He lived, in His wounded body as He died; the eyes, the brow, the scarred hands and feet, the very mien and bearing of Him; at last the Master's voice : 'Behold me, it is I Myself.'

Then that disciple whom Jesus loved believed and saw.

PART II

THE INSTRUMENT APPLIED

V

THE CREED-MAKING OF THE CHURCH UNIVERSAL

[May 7th, 1911.]

"Lo, I am with you all the days."

V

THE CREED-MAKING OF THE CHURCH UNIVERSAL

ROMANS XII. 5.—"We being many are one body in Christ."

THE point, reached now by our enquiry, at which we must turn from the study of Creed as a principle in the life of religion, to the study of those specific applications in practice which are the Creeds of the Catholic Church, is the point where sympathies will most wake and questions begin to burn. The interest felt in what happens when a man makes or keeps his private formula of belief is for every one except the man himself a speculative interest only, with which no one else, at least in our day, claims to intermeddle. What happens when it is the Church which formulates a belief and requires an open act of obedience by confession of it, is a question the answer to which is a public concern and draws with it overt consequences not in the spiritual sphere only, but in the practical sphere where there are Tests and Subscriptions, and the binding and loosing of communion.

I

What is a Creed of the Church? It is easily answered that it is a confession of faith formulated not by the individual Christian, but by the body of Christians. But in our analysis Creed is a mode of utterance, by which the confessor does the act of self-giving to an unseen Reality : and the Creed is true if there comes to him from that Reality the reciprocation which makes life for the soul of the confessor. If this analysis is correct, a Creed affirmed by the Church is an utterance in which not the individual but the body makes that self-impartment, and receives, if answer comes, the life. Yet if no more is said than this our thinking will not be advanced, and still less our religious practice guided.

For what to us, in any sense touching human conduct, is the Church?

It is a question in metaphysics and high metaphysics : for it is the question of the relation between the Universal and the Particular, asked at that level at which the Universal is Divine Reality and the Particular is a Soul of man. There is, however, a metaphysic which the humblest Christian must needs employ if he tries to think at all of this soul and its fortunes : it is this Everyman's Metaphysic which we will put in exercise.

We are, I believe, accustomed to say that not Churches are saved, but Souls. Now to say that churches are not saved may be to affirm concerning the counsels of the Creator more than we can certainly know : for it is to say that a certain social order which is now being evolved on earth cannot possibly survive as an entity in the eternal world : and that is a thing

THE CHURCH UNIVERSAL 113

which we cannot with modesty either deny positively or assert. But to say that souls are saved and not churches is a useful and impressive way of reminding us that persons and not things are the realities of existence; that 'Church' is an abstraction, the name of a relation between personal beings, the members of the Church; and that what a church does or suffers is only done and suffered by these persons. By help then of that reminder, let us define the creed of a church as a means of utterance by which the Christian lives the life of spirit, not as an individual soul, but as a social being; that is, a being whose personality is, in a great and vastly predominant measure, constituted by his relations in sentiment and conduct to a multitude of other believers like himself. So much of the man's being as is built up of these relations to the society of the Church; all that range of his existence which is parcelled out into duties to his neighbours and specially those of the household of faith, into the emotions of sympathy with all persons and causes covered by the name of Church, and into the imaginings and understandings which are his picture of the world as the kingdom of the Christ,— all this of him (and is there much else that is left him to be all his own?), all this utters itself and finds itself alive when he believes in his heart and makes confession with his mouth of a creed, which is not his but the Church's. As member of the society named the Church, he lives by this confession. That ground-law of man's existence in the world, that man is the creature of Society, has its last requirement fulfilled in the life he gains by incorporation in the Church. It is Society, the union of his parents in marriage, which brought him out of the pre-natal dark into 'the shores of light.' Society sheltered and tended the faint flame of being in the lap of a family, Society fashioned the child and the youth in the school, protected him from enemies in the tribe, enriched him and amplified his powers in the community of the city, made his intellectual being live and thrive and grow in the republic of letters and of science, and his moral being attain its stature in the fraternity of the state. And last, Society has her perfect work in the family of the household of God. That angel of God's presence, who in form and fashion of Humanity has fed man all his life long unto this day, the day of a spirit's dawning; who has redeemed him from all evil of body and of mind, from hunger and nakedness and fang of beast, from poverty and ignorance and savagery and war; that Angel still has him by the hand, and now at last unveils to show Himself as the Spirit who is Giver of life to the Church. In the City of God the spiritual being of man, by virtue of which he is 'the roof and crown of things,' is guarded, gifted, disciplined by the ministrations of the Church. Apart from Society, man, it was said, must be either beast or god, or else be nought at all: and, apart from the Church, man the spirit is also nought, or else a something more evil than nought; he must perish as a babe exposed upon the heath, or the lost tribesman

THE CHURCH UNIVERSAL 115

in the forest of the wild beast, or the lone merchantman fallen among thieves. Within the Church his spirit can live. Her truths of the divine realities nourish it, her sacraments fortify, her worships warm, her gospellings enlarge, her discipline moulds, her opportunities of service exercise to strength and tenderness, her glory nerves with loyalties, her visions that make blest inspire to sacrifice. Living to the Church he lives to Him who said, 'When ye do it unto the least of these my brethren, ye do it unto Me.' Thus is it that the corporate creed makes for our salvation: it is the means by which the soul can seek and find and avail herself of the communion of saints, which is a mediate communion with God Himself. The life which a believer can have as churchman (and how vast is its proportion in his whole of life!), this life can breathe and beat in the exercise of uttering the Church's creed.

II

How then say some among us that the believer can be a good believer without a creed, that denominational religion is a less true religion, and undogmatic Christianity is the most Christian? This contention is quite plainly in conflict with our present contention that dogma, in the form of a creed to be recited in common by churchmen, is a means, not an exclusive but an essential means, of life unto God. How do we deal with this contention, the theory of Undogmatic Christianity?

One cannot think that the justifiers of dogma choose the right line of justification when they adopt, as some do, the apologetic attitude. When the Church is charged with a needless and mischievous production of definitions, an answer frequently heard is that the Church had no desire to define the truth with this particularity, but was forced against her will to do it by the errors of the heretics which could not be left uncorrected. Thus, if she asserted at Nicaea that the Son is of one substance with the Father, it was because Arius was denying the deity of Christ, and Athanasius had no choice but to affirm it. But this he was compelled to do in a language which, while it could not truly image the unimaginable, yet was the image most near to it among conceptions attainable by men of that day. As at Nicaea so always, it is urged, the church gave the names to divine realities, not from a wish to name the unspeakable, but from the necessity of rejecting the wrong names which human error was inventing. And a favourite figure for the popularising of this view of dogma has been to speak of the 'defences of the Faith': each new dogmatic pronouncement has been not a gratuitous attempt to fasten a hard word and metaphysical theory on the mind and conscience of Christians, but to preserve a threatened truth by a new face of entrenchment thrown up to rebut a new assault.

III

This metaphor is not felicitous. To suggest that the warfare of the Christian belief is to be a defensive war, and even a fighting behind entrenchments, is of ill omen: in war the pure defensive is apt to lose; and, like other combatants, the Christian soldier must defend his cause in the open. But indeed it is not warfare, of defence or offence, which is the illuminating metaphor here. Doubtless there is to be a contending for the faith once delivered; but beside the contention of polemics, there is that of dialectics: there is the ἀγαθὴ ἔρις, the 'healthful strife,' of controversialists who strive together not for victory over the opponent, but for a conquest of truth between them through the encounter of minds. That is what the dispute of orthodoxy and heresy should often be, though it too rarely has been. We have come to recognise of late that the reproach of a heresy condemned by history may be the mis-spelt inscription over the grave of a true man, who went on honest venture in the quest of religious truth, but miscarried, because to find the truth is hard for the whole church, and for the single quester without the church a something more than hard. Would the church, however, herself have found the truth without the heretic? Was it not in the dialectic, misgrown into a polemic between her and him that the truer formulation was gendered? If no Arius had raised the question which gathered the Bishops to Nicaea, would Athanasius— or, if he, would the Catholic Church—have attained the distinct and confident vision of a Christ who was very God, of a union of man with God which is real and throughout? Perhaps. For dialectic is not the only way of the birth of truth; God is also to be known 'in solitary places, and out of the glowing intelligences which he gave to men of old;' though even so that lone intelligence is only imparted to the multitude of them that believe through a dialectic between prophet's mind and people's. But certainly, unless the gift of prophetic illumination is claimed by the apologists of dogma, they do well to think of their opposites in controversy first, and so long as they may, as fellow-seekers of truth in this 'healthful strife' where wit sharpens wit to the more knowledge of holy things. And yet, as the prevalent methods of controversy in the Church have been, and, with much softening latterly, still are, would an adoption of this attitude towards the questioners of our dogmas be less than a revolution in method?

Yet that such a dealing with questioners is a right way towards truth does seem pointed out to us by all the considerations which we have been traversing in our study of creed. If life does indeed come, as we think, by the self-uprendering interchange of that which lives and that unto which it lives, will not that vital function which is the reception of divine truths and among them of true dogma be effected by such an interchange? And if so, may not the mind of the disputant with whom our contention is, be to our own mind that special spot in our environment at which we must attempt the intercommunion through which life is born;—as again to *his* thought, if it is truth indeed, not victory, that he desires, our thought will be that Other than Self which he can touch and live?

IV

At any rate, 'Let us not to the marriage of *true* minds admit impediment,' even in dispute concerning the truth as it is in Christ Jesus. That union is to be sought not in what a disputant says, but in what he thinks. What the Undenominationalist says is that the defining of truth is an evil: what he thinks, though unwittingly, is that *wrong* defining is evil, and that the defining of the undefinable is wrong. His revolt is not against the science of theology, but against a science which is unscientific. He sees theologians laying down laws of fact, where from the state of the matter enquired into, it is not yet possible to formulate a law, as when there is pressed upon acceptance by his logical faculty some proposition about spiritual things which are spiritually, not logically, discerned. Or when theologians teach as divine doctrines the speculations of men, enforcing, for example, some theory of the Atonement, as if it were the eternal truth of the matter, when it can be no more than the best metaphor, forensic or sacrificial or other, which they have been able to find to image what is beyond imagination; and even so the best for its own day only or until a better has been inspired.

Then on his side the apologist of dogma needs to

have his true meaning discovered to the other, and, in order that this may be, needs to have it discovered first by himself. For when he makes the claim that religious belief must be definite, we who wholly assent to that pronouncement, must yet be allowed to go behind the terms of it. For he is supposed to say, and supposes himself to say, that belief must be expressed in *words* which are definite. When he protests against statements of religious truth as indefinite, vague, amorphous, invertebrate, he is applying these epithets to the *language* in which the faulty catechisms are written. And he may be right in so characterising the formulations he decries. But in this he misses the point which really matters. The language in which religion is taught ought certainly to be as definite as the circumstances may permit; but it is not the *language* of a catechism to which definiteness is essential. In 'definite church teaching' (to use a standard idiom) what must be definite is not the phrase of the teacher, but the impression stamped on the mind of the taught: in vain the clear-cut formula unless it leave clearness in the scholar's conception. No teaching, for instance, is conveyed, I suppose, with more definiteness of word than that of mathematics; but there are intellects upon which the precision of an algebraic or geometric exposition will leave no impress at all, not even of a blur. Of wisdom, no less than wit, the prosperity lies in hearer's ear, not speaker's mouth. But of the heavenly wisdom the prosperity lies not in the hearer's senses, but in his soul. There then, and no where else unless there, the definiteness of religious teaching must be achieved. How will that be? By the teaching, whether definite or vague, which stirs in the learner the movement of his soul whereby all that is within him of judgement and sympathy and force unites itself to the reality which the teacher bids his scholar know. We shall have taught the doctrine of the Fatherhood of God if, while we are speaking of it in stumbling accents, our disciple has felt move in him the instinct of adoption that cries Abba, Father: and the doctrine of the Atonement, when his heart burns in him with a blind forecast that the Saving Passion is a fact in nature, and that in very deed it is more blessed for the Self to give than to receive. This is why there have been masters in the chief of sciences, who had a scanted gift of lucidity, and yet were great doctors of the faith, because in the clouded thought and stammering utterance there went a virtue out of them: the faith in them stirred by its vibration the faith in their scholars, and the lesson echoed thus was learned.

V

We have glanced at the limitations of the disputants over the cause of Dogma. Is there some common standard against which we can measure each of them? For us that standard of measurement could be no other than the conception from which and towards which all our reflections have worked. Man's salvation is man's life unto God: faith saves him because faith is this life. But that which lives unto God is the whole man: not a part only, as those would seem to hold who suppose a man can enter into life with the right eye of his thought plucked out, or the right hand of his activity cut off and cast from him. We people of a faith which is Catholic cannot make this division of the indivisible, cannot admit a schism in the 'single state of man' who is to be saved. His salvation must be a whole salvation, a saving of his being throughout: the man must have life *semper, ubique, omnis*, not only in all time, but in all parts of him and in all of every part. But if this be so, then the undogmatic believer does greatly err who thinks to be saved without a creed; thinks that he can enter the Paradise of the life spiritual, taking with him a heart that loves and a will that serves the Almighty, and leaving outside the pale that organ of his being through which he can know God by His holy Name, and can give, like the first man in earth's paradise, names to each of God's creatures, and among these creatures to each Godward thought and emotion which has a being in his soul. And the champion of a dogmatic Christianity also errs, though for the most part in theory only, theory which his practice betters, when he speaks as if one part of man, his reasoning faculty, could save the whole. For that is what is said, though far indeed from what is thought and farther yet from what is acted on, when he says that it is 'before all things necessary to salvation that a man hold the catholic faith'; and then—then—says that 'the catholic faith' which is to save the man 'is this'; is the form of words that follow thereupon. 'Before all things necessary.' Can it be that? Can it be first and most in the fortunes of the living soul of a man that a form of words, however sound and healthful words, yet a form and of words, should be recited by him with assent? Can this be the head and front of our redeeming from the everlasting loss? Can it be a perfect counselling of the soul to name as first the care of one strand in the triple cord of life, the strand of reason, and leave the strand of action not named except in a brief syllable at parting, and that of love not acknowledged by even one bare syllable of a name? It is not a perfect counselling, while it is left thus unguarded, with no warning of its partialness of intent, which might comfort simple souls, who feel the imperfectness, but, being simple, give that feeling some name that does it wrong. They think themselves and are thought to be denying the catholic faith, when they are but hungering for the whole of faith, and discontent that for the whole they are offered a third.

It is of these simple folk that we are thinking, when we plead that the apologist of dogma should meet the rejecter of dogma in the spirit, not of polemic, but of dialectic. We are thinking of the simple who says in his mind 'There is no name I can give to God,' not of the fool who hath said in his heart, 'There is no God to whom a name can be given.' Too readily the dogmatist confounds these two. Let him distinguish.

For when iron sharpeneth iron, where humble dogmatist and honest undenominationalist are countenance to countenance; when selfless heart and open mind and ready will of both join, by a mutual sacrifice of each to other, in a common sacrifice to the Very Truth; the spark will fall from heaven, and between them will spring alight the faith.

How that mutual faith of the two in union will differ from the faith which each had in his isolation, we have forecast already by our criticism of the two attitudes. We may give this forecast a summary form, by saying that what the two will learn between them concerning belief and salvation is this. Since living—and not seeing—is believing, we may not hope that a belief will save us, if to believe is only to see with a mind's eye the truth of a creed. And since not part of us, but all, needs to be saved, we may not hope for salvation if the mind that makes creed be left unsaved. Soul is not saved by the mind, and soul is not saved without it. How undeniable by either disputant! By both how unremembered!

VI

But now out of this same 'Living is Believing,' and out of the repugnancy of undogmatic religionists to our dogmas, because they seem to these to be not living but dead, comes a question charged with most anxious issues. Faith is life unto God, we say, and of this life creeds are to be ministers. But life comes only from life, and a creed that is to give life must

THE CHURCH UNIVERSAL 125

be alive. How then if a creed of the Church should be not alive but dead? Or, since that question is, though ideally possible, yet hardly a real one, how if a creed, which is itself a living body, should have a dead member in it? What can we do about such a mortified limb?

It is a question which will not be spared us in our dialectic with the 'undogmatic Christian,' for his difficulty is that parts of the Church's formularies are for him not alive. Shall we then answer, as is usual with maintainers of credal religion, that first the creeds are not dead, and then that they cannot die : that they were framed by the catholic church, still undivided, and therefore throughout all her frame still 'the spirit-bearing body,' still assured of truth in her judgements through Christ in the midst?

It is our confident belief that this answer is a true answer,—if only it understands itself. Our attempt will be to examine whether this condition—a right understanding of their answer—is always fulfilled in those who put it to use. There is much need to ask ourselves afresh, on occasion of the challenge of our comrades in this dialectic, what we mean by the terms catholic church and catholicity, what by the authority of Councils, what by Tradition and the Deposit of Faith, by Antiquity, Continuity with the Primitive Church, Succession from the Apostles.

VII

We shall most compendiously study this by consideration of a formula of great prestige in which is crystallised as it were the theory of catholicity most accepted in our church. This is the apophthegm of Vincent of Lerinum, that we must hold as of Catholic faith 'that which has been believed everywhere, always, by all.' It has seemed to many among us that the canon of *Ubique, semper, ab omnibus* rules out of all hope any change in such definitions of the faith as possess these notes of catholicity. For such definitions, notably in the Nicene Creed, have come down to us from an age in which the requirements of that canon were fulfilled. There was once an undivided church, able to agree upon a creed, and by that church creeds were framed which did obtain this universality of belief. There is an undivided church no longer, and the divisions are so many and so deep that the whole church can do nothing as a whole; cannot meet in council, and there, with Christ's spirit in the midst, apprehend a truth which all men everywhere shall assent to and recognise as having been in all time the belief of Christians. The endowment of Catholic truth which has descended to the present dismembered kingdom of Christ from the centuries of the Church's wholeness is therefore incapable of addition: the foundation on which she must support herself is the wealth of experience capitalised in these few centuries only: the Sparta which has fallen to her lot may seem a narrow one and an austere, but her lot it is, and this she must order as best she may.

Does Vincent's Canon really consign us to this straitness? Let us look at it closely. It is impressive enough to match its greatness in history, but not transparently clear. At a first glance one might think its logic is at fault, for it has the look of the logical fault of cross-division, or at least the blemish of tautology. If a thing is believed everywhere and always, why add that it is believed by all men; this *ab omnibus* seems to repeat the *ubique* and the *semper*. Are we to charge Vincent with slovenliness in so critical and momentous a formulation? No: one looks again, and the logic has emerged with a brilliant instructiveness. Vincent was thinking of the Christian world he knew, Christian Europe. If a belief were found to have been held in all preceding generations, and to be exhibited in all bounds of the present territory of Christendom, yet this *Semper* and *Ubique* would not be convincing notes of Catholic truth till a third note made itself recognised. This belief, he feels, may have been held always; universality in time may be predicated of it: but how if at any one point in time it has been held indeed, but held faintly, only by few. Again, it may be at all times held everywhere, and universality in space can be claimed: but how if this spread of the belief were but a thin film covering the surface of the Everywhere, but not going below the surface? This is not enough for Vincent. ' Not all my France must hold it, but all the Christians in France; not the Bishops and Doctors only, while the lay people hold it not, nor the lay people only and not the learned too.' The faith should be found not merely everywhere in the body corporate of believers, but also with a real specific density at every point. This he expresses in quantitative language by saying it must have been believed 'by all,' from the Doctors at the top to the simple folk on the lowest stratum.

VIII

It is, however, not to the science of Numbers, but to the most contrasted one, that we shall go to interpret Vincent. May it be here recalled how in an earlier lecture it was ventured that this third dimension of Intensity was to be identified with the principle of Life itself? We are suggesting that this principle, which came to us by simple observation of natural fact and not by memory of the theologian's canon, is what really has inspired the truth which Vincent has expressed in the rude mathematical figures supplied to him by the logic of his time. If we are jealous of this Doctor's credit, we shall not understand his canon as if it prescribed an arithmetical measurement of truth, as if truth were true because it seemed so to the multitude, and catholicity could be decided by a count of votes. Vincent was not anticipating that statesman of recent times, who said that all the people can be deceived for some time and some people for all time, but not all people for all time. For only note how he presently escapes out of mathematical into vital ideas. 'What shall the true Catholic do, if some particular Church shall have cut itself off from the communion of the universal faith? What surely but prefer the soundness of the whole body to a diseased and corrupt limb of it?' 'The whole body,' the 'diseased limb,'—there is the very truth of the matter, though it springs to light incidentally. It is not the undividedness and totality of the body of the Church which makes it Catholic : it is the health and soundness of it; not the wholeness but the haleness, which is but changed spelling for the same word. Now healthy, sound, uncorrupt, whole or hale, these are so many synonyms for 'living,' as diseased and corrupt are names of dying and dead. Here is the secret of it all. 'Catholic,' though it is Greek for English 'whole,' and in etymology identical with it, is greater and better than whole, as the cause is more than what it causes. Catholicity in the Church is the Life which makes the Church a whole. As in a living creature the wholeness of its body is the oneness of it, and the oneness is made solely by the life which beats in it from centre to circumference; as the limb mortified by the damming back of the life-streams is, as Vincent tells us, a limb severed from the whole; as the complex frame, 'wonderfully made,' of bone and sinew and tissue, which we call an organic body, is, once the mystic fire of life is blown out, not a body, but a heap of earth-matter crumbling back into unfeatured dust;—even so is it with the life spiritual. The wholeness or catholicity of the Church is indeed her oneness and undividedness; but that oneness is the life in her, which we name the indwelling of Christ or of the Spirit of Christ; and that soul or that church into which the life flows not, is no part now of the catholic whole, not because it is severed, but because it has died or is dying. And this mighty frame of Christendom, if the Lord who is Giver of Life should depart from His temple, would keep in vain, if it kept at all, the stately and subtle frame of catholic creed, catholic sacramental system, catholic order: for it would be One no more. As a corpse sinks into its dust, it would have sunk back from the One in Many, Many in One, which is Christ's Body the Church, into the Many which are not the One, but are the Nought.

IX

How known and old a truth is this! And how needing to be known!

For out of it comes what? There comes the answer to every question which tries the heart of the Catholic Christian. There comes the warrant of the divine right by which priest rules and pastor ministers righteousness; there comes the title-deed by which bishop inherits Apostle; there comes the security by which it is known that sacraments have virtue to heal and save; there comes the inspiration by which the scribe instructed unto the kingdom of heaven brings out from the treasure of Holy Scripture the things old of the Letter and the things new of Interpretation; there comes the law by the guidance of which the

THE CHURCH UNIVERSAL 131

Church has power to decree rite and ceremony, to maintain the old uncorrupt, to sanction or condemn the newly-forged, to recall the suspended into use, to proclaim in ritual controversy peace to them that are near and peace to them that are far off, peace to the contenders for a Use and to the contenders against it, the peace of Christ who is our Life and makes us one; there comes the pure and holy casuistry by which the formula of a test is interpreted and the conscience of the subscribing priest is taught; there comes the guidance for the Church's rulers, by which they can wisely bind and loose; and there come the best regulatives for the crowded, jostling march of our social evolution, and the clearest light upon the lone path of the single soul.

All these things come out of the truth that Catholicity is life. And with these there comes, last, not because it is least nor yet most, but because it is that which we are now setting out to judge, there comes the right of a Branch of Christ's Church to study, by herself and not in council with the rest with whom her communion is no longer full, the ancient inherited creeds which are both hers and theirs; to study them afresh with her own living intelligence, so that it be also with the mind which she has in her of Christ; to study them, and to re-judge. Yes, to re-judge. We must not fear the word, as if it were presumptuous. For indeed the duty of judging the creed we profess is part, and an inseparable part, of the duty of professing it. Judge we must in any case, for if to find a formula inadequate is a judgement, so also to confirm the formula is a judgement of it. And the judgement is one which must take effect. If when a Particular Church has studied her creed, taking counsel in the light of a spiritual communion brooding over her as the wings of a dove, if she finds its language, so studied, to be all-sufficient and able to bring forth in her the fruits of knowledge and strength and love, then she is assured that in her creed she is Catholic; Christ is her Father, though some Abraham of the earliest Christian past be ignorant of her, and the Israel of some stately sister-communion acknowledge her not. But also, if it should be revealed to her by the Spirit that, among those ancient words of mortal language which framed her old-time knowledge of God, are any words which were once potent ministers of faith and life, but have outlived this potency and are even cumberers of faith, unless the Spirit touch them into life again :—if this should be, then, in the power of this truth that Catholicity is the Divine Life in a church, and Catholic belief is belief which is alive by Christ that liveth in it, a branch of the Church may venture to re-interpret or even to re-mould the language of her creeds; and this action—or, in the other case, the refusal of action—if only it be an act of life unto Christ in God, shall have the name and the worth of Catholic.

X

'Yet I believe,' a churchman may say, 'in one Catholic and *Apostolick* Church : in a deposit of faith handed down by tradition. This is forgotten in your interpretation of Catholic.'

But the Deposit of Faith—what is it? The Tradition—by what means do we hand it on?

For many of us the Deposit of which each age is trustee has meant the creeds and credal institutions of the Church; the Word, Sacraments, Order. It is all these : but it is out of all proportion more. Not the creed of Christendom, but the life with which Christ endowed His Church is the trust put in our keeping. This life, unless all our reasonings have been idle, is not a name for a mystery embraced by a vague emotion, but for a reality having substance, form, and feature; a fact that can be recognised and in some degree even measured. We can know whether this life is in us or is not, and therefore can know whether the Church has kept safe her trust and is transmitting it unabated and unspoiled.

By what means does the Church transmit it? By Word, Sacrament, and Discipline. By nothing else?

Well, many perhaps have so supposed. In a long controversy over religious education in the school, how dominant, though unconsciously, has been the assumption that if we can teach a creed we shall convey a faith. When it was remembered that besides definite teaching there must also be demanded 'atmosphere,' an environment of social influence inspired by religion, it was a timely recall from a misdirection: we had reminded ourselves that creed and catechism alone do not make Christians. No, for Christians are not made; they are born.

And their birth is on this wise. We call the Church our Mother; she bears children unto Christ. That is no figure; it is the utter fact. As the human parents engender the child of their flesh not by creation of a life, but by transmission of a life entrusted to themselves, so the church genders her children. She lives the life unto Christ, and the new souls brought into contact with her act of life are born alive to Christ: are born alive not because they have received a word, but because they have touched a power; not because a creed was taught them, but because a faith set their faith afire.

Watch it happen. Go with Peter to the house of Cornelius, and note how the Church engendered her children then. Did Peter make those men Christians by a creed? Not without one indeed, for the tale of Jesus slain and risen was a creed. But do we think the story of a martyred Prophet's return to life worked the conversion? Admiration, pathos, wonder it might work; not the surrender of self to the Divine, which is faith. No, the life that was in the speaker touched the hearers and life was lit in them. There was happening in him, as he spoke, the sacrifice of self, which is kindled by the fire from heaven. The love that went and came between Peter and his Lord burned before his listeners as he spoke the things of Christ;

burned not only or even most in the words which framed his story, but in the flame of a conviction, a passion, a resolve, that streamed out in the accent on the lip, the light quickening in the eye, and all that nameless irradiation by which the spirit of a man transpires to those who mark him. But those who marked Peter, let us remember this, were men capable of that spiritual reception. They were not unawakened Syrian peasants, nor religionists of the 'hard church'; they were men 'whose hearts God had opened.' To this opened heart of seeker there is offered in the tale of Peter the spectacle of the world-secret, that by sacrifice comes not death, as seems to mortals, but, as seen in Jesus, Life. But this spectacle—here lies the truth we are aiming at—came home to their heart and will not by force of the record of a past human incident (though not without that record), but by force of the visible happening of an incident in the present, the narrator's own act of faith wrought before their very eyes in his telling of the tale. 'While Peter yet spoke these words, the Holy Ghost fell on all them which heard the word.' These listeners felt happen in themselves the like act of faith: they too made the self-surrender to God in Christ; their souls were born alive.

XI

This was the manner of the tradition of the faith which had been once delivered unto Peter. The same had been the manner of the delivery of the faith to

Peter's self. Not the doctrine which Jesus taught made this disciple receive the faith; not this, but the life unto the Father which lived in Jesus, the spectacle of a life laid down and taken again. In the contact with that life the first disciple's soul was born alive : and by contact with the fire of sacrifice lit in him the fire kindled again in these.

And we maintain the Apostolicity of the Tradition, when we transmit, as did the Apostles, the life that is from Christ. For that transmission there are instruments, and among them is 'the form of sound words' in which the Church came to tell more elaborately what Peter told with brief simplicity. But this form of words was not Peter's, and not in it is stored the force by which Peter's work upon his brethren's souls was wrought. It costs more to redeem their souls.

What then, we have to ask, what is that 'more'? To know it matters all in all. The knowledge of creed, doctrine, sacrament, ritual, order, is a knowledge briefly comprehended in this Something More, this faith that makes faith again. This it is that a church must minister where she ministers a creed, if she would prove herself true branch of the Church which is Catholic and Apostolic. What is this Something More?

VI

THE CREED-MAKING
OF THE CHURCH PARTICULAR

[May 14th, 1911]

"Where two or three are gathered together in my name, there am I in the midst of them."

VI

THE CREED-MAKING
OF THE CHURCH PARTICULAR

1 Cor. xii. 27.—"Now ye are the body of Christ, and members in particular."

I

THE position has been taken up in our foregoing argument, that a Branch of the Church Catholic is able not only to decree rites and ceremonies for the good of her members, but also to revise her creeds and to re-affirm or to re-formulate. Further, that although she cannot in this divided Christendom take counsel with the whole church, yet her act can be catholic, if it is an act of life unto God in Christ; and that, although she may depart from the word of the Apostolic tradition, yet she will have discharged her trust faithfully, if she has transmitted the life unto God which is the matter of the tradition.

In this, however, lies all. If we shall have so far prospered in our reasonings as to persuade those loyal and reverent minds in our communion who are most zealous for the faithfulness to its trust, that the catholicity of a church consists in no quantitative relation, that her 'universality' is no matter of numbers, areas, and periods, but of the Spirit, the timeless and spaceless, who dwelleth in her; that this indwelling of the Spirit has its demonstration in the life that beats in this living organism the Church, whether the Church as spread through the wide world of the Ecumenè, or the Church as islanded in the narrow bound of a self-dependent communion,—still they will object that this test of life is an instrument which we cannot use. 'You tell us,' they will say, 'that the making or re-making of a Creed must be an act of life. But what is the way of such an act: what function of what organ in Christ's Body the Church is the function of living? And if there be such an organ and such a function of it, how can we know that this functioning has taken place and the organ has lived? A written Creed which has descended from the past is a plain unchanging standard against which we can set a new thought and ascertain agreement or divergence: but this "Life" is a vague, immeasurable thing which cannot be the measure of anything. As well might one estimate the height of a tree by comparison not with a neighbouring tower, but with the cloud carried past it. How then invite us to exchange the test of definite written words for the impalpabilities of this principle of life? The ship of the church has lain these many centuries safely moored from a shipwreck against the rocks of Doubt, while her anchor has been cast in the sure holding ground of ancient creeds which record the once-delivered faith. Shall we now, for fear lest, under the winds of Criticism, this anchor should drag and throw us on the reef, dare to pull it in, and trust to our mere seamanship with sail and rudder to ride the peril out? Is this "life," so vast, elusive, and immeasurable, a thing with which a Church can trust her soul?'

Indeed that is well asked: and it needs to be answered well.

Yet first it must be said, though we cannot stay to make it good, that the choice is not between anchorage in the Past and our own seamanship. The anchor drags. The Church does not trust her soul, nor did she ever trust it, to the anchorage of 'It is written,' if it were only written and were not also read, marked, learned, and inwardly digested, and so made life in the believer. If the principle here advocated be a seamanship, those who mistrust it must still provide some other.

II

We are then to show that the fashioning of a creed by a Particular church can be an act of life, and that it can be known whether the church lives in doing it.

This requires that we should carefully picture to our mind the process of a creed-making. The picture can best be constructed by the study of some historical instance. There is one which is the classical instance, the creed-making of the fourth century by the two first General Councils and the half century of struggle which came between them. In this action of the Church Universal we may read, writ large, the act of a Church Particular.

What is the picture? As drawn for us by history it is the flocking of three hundred bishops to hear the cause of the advocates who impugn and the advocates who defend the Divinity of Jesus Christ, and to judge which of these has the truth. Three hundred Over-Shepherds, but for the most part a very simple shepherd folk, innocent of metaphysic, even in its theologic branch, and practised not in the making, but only the administration of the faith. These men are asked to weigh out Arius and Athanasius, and with a practical unanimity they decide to affirm with the latter the clause which declares the Son to be of one substance with the Father. In technical language they promulge the Homoöusion. When they have done this, has the Church decreed an article of Catholic belief? That question is answered by the fifty years of strife, of insurgent Arianism, hours when *ingemuit totus orbis et Arianum se esse miratus est* (Jerome); fallings away of timid moderates from the side of Athanasius, left lone against the world as Elijah, and after a like Carmel victory; Athanasius tossed to and fro, from home to exile, exile to home, and back again and back, on the clashing tides of a warfare in which politics seem all but all, and faith only not nothing: fifty years of strife, and then—Constantinople. The seven thousand in Israel who would not bow the knee to that earthly image of a Christ who was less than Very God of Very God, who would not consent to the low destiny of man which matched that low thought of man's Redeemer, hearts

THE CHURCH PARTICULAR 143

whose 'greatness did not fail through craven fear of being great,'—these men have now in their following the holy catholic Church wheresoever spread throughout the world. What the Clerus in their council at Nicaea had promulged, that the Populus in the council of the wide world has accepted. The dogma that the Son is of one substance with the Father, the truth that God has verily and indeed made human nature capable of union with His own, this is now the Catholic faith. For the Church throughout the world has travailed—with what pangs of labour : *ingemuit totus orbis*!—and this is the truth she has brought to birth. *Judicavit orbis terrarum* : and that judgement is sure.

III

When we seek by aid of a humane imagination, to which history gives up more of its secret, to see deeper into this picture of a judgement by the *orbis terrarum*, we find ourselves in converse with a range of facts very different in complexion from those which the historian has to handle. Instead of debates in council halls, motions, votes, and pronouncements, intrigue, agitation, impeachments, depositions, excommunications, things which can be registered in records, our converse must be with facts multitudinous, minute, homely, human, insignificant, with the infinity of the thinkings, feelings, and doings of private men, which in their sum are the total mind and will of Christendom. We look upon a vasty sea-surface of human consciousness, its welter of indistinguishable wavelets, an ocean's 'innumerable smile,' or frown, in response to unseen forces which draw or agitate or smoothe again the immensity of its waters. This infinitude of human stories of men and women of no account is the true history of how a faith is formulated. The stories are not to be read on the written page, as we can read how Athanasius hides for his life, how Arius expires on his way to a triumph; which emperor succoured one champion, and which the other; what votes were cast in council for this cause and for that. Yet there is a chemistry by which we can restore this vanished writing: it is the light and warmth of an imaginative sympathy. By it we can decipher at least this much, that these men framed their creed, as each of us to-day frames his own, by living it, and finding that it brought them life. When was it otherwise? Two men come from a prison gate to question a prophet in a Galilean market town, 'Art thou he that should come?' and they carry back the answer, 'This is verily the Christ, for he works life in men: in the blind, the deaf, the lame, the dead? And even so this multitude of the fourth century addressed their question to the Christ presented to them in the Council's word,—a Christ who is the God-Man, human flesh made one with divine Spirit. Art thou he that should come? Art thou our humanity's hope? That must be seen by all and each of us. And it will be seen by me, says each one, when I have learnt whether this word they offer me is life-giver to me. I am layman and not learned clerk, and I ask for no say in theology; but I have a touch on things, if not on words, and I will know whether this belief in a God made flesh is a power upon things or a shadow among their solids. I am trader, and understand good business: in the exchanges of the moral life are they wise money-changers, as Jesus bade his disciples be, who traffic in this belief, and do they reap their interest in it? I am statesman; does it counsel me in rule? Thinker; does it point me to the secret of the world's order? Poet; does it illumine the world's beauty? I am working man; what glory does it lend my coarse labour, what delivery from my coarse lusts? I am a master's slave; is there a liberty wherewith no lesser Christ than this can set me free? I am a sufferer: if this word is medicine, if it makes all my bed in sickness, then it shall be my faith. I am woman; but they say that in Christ Jesus there is neither male nor female: if a God-Man so betters my estate, then the God-Man he is the Lord, my Lord. I am mother, sighs one: does it help me to be mother indeed to know that of a woman was born a Holy One? I am child yet, whispers another; but it makes me 'full of growing' to be told that son of Mary was son of God and increased in wisdom and stature,—as shall not I? I am girl that will be woman and may be wife; is it true that in such an one can dwell the eternal purity, eternal love? I am boy that shall be man and must be strong: I will know if what they say is true, and a spirit of counsel and of strength is in me out of heaven to make me fearless unto death.

K

Such is the picture, drawn not by formal history, but only by the power to re-construct to vision an unrecorded past, and authorised by our belief that man has always been man and his relation to spiritual things the same of old as now,—such is the picture we offer of the Church formulating a creed. In such ways, as we suppose, the Populus of the Church under the Empire weighed, judged, and at last accepted the decree Homoöusion; the multitudinous conscience of the world bearing witness and the thoughts of the innumerable Obscure accusing or else excusing between themselves a formula which the few in their council had propounded. Do we not correctly summarise this diffused moral activity of the multitude by calling it a vast experiment of the body corporate, the vast experiment in living by a truth thus offered to their consciousness. To the stimulus of a creed's claim on their adherence the wide organism of the household of Christ attempted to make response. In that response came to them animation, an animation of each one's living self. The doubting found assurance, the struggling by their patience won their soul, the timid had courage, the lame walked, the deaf heard, the blind received sight, and to the poor—this above all—to the poor in wealth or wit or opportunity a Gospel which could save was preached. The Church Universal made this creed, 'The Son is of one substance with the Father,' by an action of its whole being which was an act of living unto God.

IV

But, while we summarise the vast process, let us also articulate it. It will presently assist us in our application of the ancient example to modern instances, if we note that the far-extended action by which this creed was made divides itself into the two plainly distinguished moments, that of the promulgation at Nicaea and that of the acceptance in the Ecumenè. The process of creed-making which we desire to study in our own times is writ large for us not merely by the grand scale on which is deployed the Nicene controversy, but also by this so legible distinctness of the two moments, the debates of the *clerus* in council and the fifty years' agitation of the *populus*. For that articulation seems to be a psychological law of the Church's dealing with creeds; and this structural law will be more easily traced in the perplexed phenomenon of a formulative act done by a modern church, if we have viewed it first in the Nicene example as in a norm.

In that example the promulgation and the acceptance embodied in actual history the two ideal stages, which faith, whether individual or corporate, must pass through. Faith must begin in venture and end in realisation, just as knowledge begins in hypothesis and is completed in verification.

It is plain that the action of the Council was a venture. To a company of men who were not practised reasoners about their faith the question is put, 'What think ye of Christ? Whose Son is He? Is

He the Son of God and nothing less?' They answer, 'He is. For when we examine our conscience we find such has been our thought and the thought of our flocks; we have lived our lives on this assumption, though, being simple men and not philosophers, we have not tested it with any logic, but only tried it against our heart and our people's hearts. When Athanasius declares that Christ is Very God, our experience echoes him. Our spirits bear witness to it, and the Spirit who helpeth our infirmities He witnesses with us. Yea, it is so: Christ is God.'

In the colder speech of this day it would be said, they bare the witness of an instinct, they saw the truth by an intuition. Also it can be said, as we have phrased it, they confessed the faith by a venture. Else the Incarnation truth would not have been achieved: nothing ventured had been nothing won.

There followed the people's moment, the realisation by experiment. A moment it is, though it measures fifty years.

To the eye of one who reads only such facts as can find place in chronicles, there may be presented a spectacle unsanctified enough, and liable to the sneer of history. He will recognise only a random seething embroilment of churchmen and men of state, in a war, under sacred emblems, of worldly passions and blind violences. But, to the sense which spiritually discerns things spiritual, this scene of an empire's corporate consciousness seeking to respond to the stimulus of a truth wherever that truth made contact with the myriad minute experiences of common men and women, will rather be the scene of a pouring out of the Spirit upon all flesh, a secret descending and dividing among the multitude of them that believed of an inspiration's ghostly fire, a conviction that sat upon each of them. So to speak of it is not to use the elated language of a pious fancy, seeing in the dark of the past not what is there but what it wishes should be there. There are indications few, but not disproportionately few, on the scant page of written history, that in the thought and conduct of the rank and file of churchmen there was, in answer to the leadership of the recorded few, a serious and sincere contention for the faith. This should enable us to discern in the people's assent to the Council's pronouncement no mere secular movement manœuvred by the forces of nature or of statecraft, but a demonstration of Spirit and of power.

V

How then does this creed-making by the whole church light up the problem of creed-making by a Particular Church? The structural lines discovered in the admittedly catholic procedure will reappear in the action of the Branch, though with a difference. In our own communion, to which we may here confine our attention, the two moments of Promulgation and Acceptance are in practice fused, but in principle remain. The Council of the Fourth Century has at present no true equivalent in the Twentieth, nor indeed could possibly, in our democratised society, have an exact counterpart, even after a hoped-for reconstitution of our church's legislature. But then the conciliar function of promulging is only a particular mode of the function of leadership in thought; and without leadership no body of men can formulate a thought. A formulary may, like a proverb, be the wisdom of many men, as indeed we have just now been arguing that it is: but as certainly it is one man's wit. A leader must find the word of the common faith, the multitude must find that it is the true word. The conciliar and the popular parts may be, in appearance, merged in a debate where the two Houses, as it were, of the Clerus and the Populus discuss and resolve as one in common session; but the two distinct parts will still be sustained, and creeds be still made, as was the earliest of all, by a Peter who confesses 'Thou art the Christ' and a brotherhood of disciples who assent that so do they believe.

We do not need to construct imaginatively the procedure of our church when it gives shape to a confession. She has done it more than once in the knowledge of our generation. For there are beliefs held by the church which have found no statement in any formal creed, yet are as substantial and as operative on thought and conduct as many articles of a formulary. Two such beliefs we have seen remodelled by our generation, the old theory of Verbal Inspiration of Scripture, and the theory involved in it of a Six Days' Creation. These articles of faith

THE CHURCH PARTICULAR 151

were extra-credal, but they were defended, when attacked by the criticism of that day, with an energy which confessed that in the mind of the church at large they ranked in value with the positive creeds. These articles the church has reformulated, and she does not doubt that her actions was catholic. What then was the method which this reform pursued?

The method was an effort of churchmen to readjust themselves to an intellectual environment suddenly changed, to make new and fit response to the stimulus of new facts, such as the enlarged distances, temporal and spacial, of the universe, or the actualities of the sacred literature's production. Men of science and of scholarship declared these facts, and the general consciousness of churchmen repelled their doctrines for a while as heresies: the new discovery of how God made the world and those who tenant it did not lack a Galileo to suffer in that less stringent question-chamber of our wiser time, the court of general opinion. For in that court was the cause heard and judged. No Convocation, no Synod of Bishops promulged by authority a revised article of belief and sent it to the provinces for their assent. The pleading and counter-pleading were heard in the open, equal street of public discussion through the agencies of pulpit, press, and conference, of speech, lecture, magazine article, letters in journals, conversation in private circles, teachings of philosopher or of catechist. Here and there were cardinal moments when some pronouncement by a leading mind in book or sermon started a fresh crystallisation of fluid opinion in the masses; and always went forward the long, long, insensibly-graded process of mental and moral growth, declaring itself in some last 'unimaginable touch of time' at which the general mind of the Church awoke, without a start, to find faith unchanged but faith's word transmuted. One year we all believed that the Holy Spirit wrote with a mortal's pen the very phrase of Scripture, and it was sacrilege to think any syllable of a prophecy or even any cipher of a record on its page could err; but there came a year when we smiled at that old simplicity, and agreed that

> "every fiery prophet of old time,
> When God made music through him, could but speak
> His music by the framework and the chord,"

yet that God's the music still was, and still by his Spirit was the Bible writ. One year we listened under this pulpit, as under many another, to hear a biologist's theory denounced as faith's betrayal: and now we chide that timid imagination of ours which hindered us to conceive that God fulfils Himself in many ways, and not only in the way of our first ignorance of His power. What had happened? In council of the whole body of the faithful we had reformulated the articles of our belief touching Holy Writ and the Origin of Man. In council of the whole body. But we can discriminate here, as in the fourth century, the functions of faith's venture and faith's realisation by experience. The venture was of the stronger hearts that 'feared and were enlarged' at the challenge of new facts in the soul's environment, and ventured to promulgate their own new understanding of God, as one to whom the thousand years are as one day in the making of man, as one who can make His meanings clear to mortal sense, though He chooses to speak them through a mortal's faltering memory and stammering lips. And the realisation—that was our part, the many. We tested the offered thought which claimed to be a truer truth, against our living souls, and noted whether they languished at that touch or rather quickened. This refashioned article of an inspiration not verbal yet an inspiration, or of a heaven and earth made by evolution and yet the work of God's fingers, is it (one asked oneself) a savour of death to my faith? And one answered that 'It is a savour of life unto life; it is a freeing and widening of my being, God has set my feet in a large room, this more spacious world, where yet I find my Spirit still at home. It is strength to me and comfort: for if man from so low has been brought so high, surely the spirit of the mighty God is in him, and in this weakness of mine His strength can be made perfect: surely God was in this place of human flesh and I knew it not.'

So was made faith's venture by the few, faith's experiment by the many. Was the resulting confession a heretical opinion, or a right article of Catholic belief? Our church thinks the latter, even if here and there some true churchman still stands somewhat forlornly aloof, saying the old wine is better : she has refashioned the creed outside the creeds, and has done it by the experience that so believing she had life.

Would she have had that life without so believing? There is a sister church which has hitherto refused, and is at this time emphatically refusing, so to believe, and to refashion in the light of a new knowledge an old scholastic interpretation of the world. Is she by that refusal gaining life? Do her teachings promise to obtain by consequence a wider range over the intelligence of Christendom, or her spiritual influence more command even over simple hearts? If we have to judge that to refuse to reformulate an article has been a loss of life to our sister communion, our own action stands confirmed by the method of difference.

VI

These instances, however, of extra-credal beliefs which the Church has reformed will seem to lack instructiveness, as being, it will be said, of another genus than the articles of a primitive creed. They are of another genus no doubt on the theory of a closed Apostolic tradition, a deposit of defined belief to be transmitted intact without subtraction or addition by the later church. That is the theory which we are sifting, with expectation that our search will restore us this truth of Apostolicity with a deeper meaning and more fertility of helpfulness. But meanwhile it will seem in point to remind ourselves that in one instance we have reformulated a part even of a primitive creed. The clause 'He descended into hell' has been reformed, though tacitly, by the general consciousness of our church. When we recite it to-day we are not confessing the belief which its framers and its reciters till of late confessed. The Harrowing of Hell pictured with so grotesque a realism on medieval church-walls, is an event for which we recognise no more valid authority than a Christian's speculation about the state of the departed which has found a moment's light notice in the Scriptures. We teach our children to understand the clause as a parable of the reality of the death of Jesus, of His passage by a real dissolution of soul and body, into the spiritual existence. We have, that is, reformulated the clause by allegory. Not a letter has been changed, but the clause is a new one. Yet it is a Catholic member of the Catholic creed : and it has been formulated as such by the same activity of the common church consciousness, as that which has reformed the extra-creedal beliefs in a verbally inspired Bible and a six days' creation.

VII

We shall bring with us from these examples a greater lucidity and sureness of tread to problems which are actual for us. How shall we do about a creed, ancient though scarcely primitive, about the treatment of which there is much division of opinion in our church at this time : how shall we act about the Quicunque in a way which shall be catholic?

Our deliberations on the conflicting proposals to modify it by excision of certain clauses or to retain it intact, and the proposals to repeal or to confirm the obligatory public use, can these deliberations be so conducted that, when one or the other conclusion has been reached, we shall be sure that the faith once delivered unto the saints has been guarded by us uncorrupt?

Let it be said, as on an earlier occasion, that we are pleading here the cause not primarily and expressly of a truth, but of a method of seeking truth. Our aim is not to prove right the one or the other view in this controversy, but to show that there exists an instrument by which we can assure our hearts, that we have made our decision by the Spirit who dwelleth in the Church and us. The advocate of this method must therefore plead his cause with both parties to this question, and beg them both to let no controversial interest in that question obstruct, confuse, or divert the course of that enquiry, which is our true concern here, as to whether our method is a valid one and of practical service in theology and in faith.

The enquiry divides itself into the two questions given us by the very structure of our idea of Life. We must ask first, 'Is the church's decision for the one or the other treatment of the Quicunque an act of sacrifice?' and then, 'Does that sacrifice meet with God's acceptance, that divine partaking in it which makes the act of sacrificing an act of living unto God?'

The sacrifice. It is not difficult to indicate what

the things are of which we must make oblation on this side and on the other of the controversy. They will be the prejudices which may block the intelligence against truth's entry, and the predilections which chain the activity from its due forth-goings. What upholder of an existing order has no selfishness to fear, which is against the open mind and the ready will? His championship of antiquity is loyalty, yet perhaps not all loyalty, but in part that desire of fixity and mental rest which an English philosopher noted as a foe of secular science; and in part a clannishness of the churchman's mind defending his church's practice because it is his church's, as a patriot might cleave to 'my country, right or wrong.' Again, what repealer of a use is beyond the temptings of that pride of life, to which the zest of change, of freedom, of adventure, of reason's self-sufficingness, of the delight of mental battle with the dignified Past for adversary, gives food and stimulus? Here are materials to lay upon the altar of that sacrifice by which we inaugurate our council over our church's estate, and plead for heaven's blessing and inspiration. It can be known whether this sacrifice is offered by us or withheld. It may be objected perhaps that each churchman's action is an inward fact, known only to each. Still we believe that a society of men organised as a nation can have a corporate consciousness and not only a multitude of individual consciousnesses, that a people can know what as a people it thinks and resolves. No otherwise we must believe that a society which is a church can do the same, and therefore can know whether in a corporate deliberation the body corporate has made a sacrifice or has kept it back.

VIII

The oblation has been laid then on the altar: but the sacrifice which prospers is the sacrifice which is answered from heaven. Man's self-giving may perish fruitless, an error and a waste, if it fails of the self-giving of God, which makes it life. Can we know whether our altar burns; whether by her decision to bind or to loose the church becomes more alive?

A phenomenon so complex and subtle as that of vitality in a body corporate will be most hopefully studied if we narrow our observation to a concrete and particular case. I would propose therefore that we try to follow with sympathy the experience of some average member of the church when he uses this creed, and judge whether that use brings vitality to his individual faith and in what measure. If it is life to him, then it may well be life to the Church.

And we will imagine this churchman to be one whom the upholders of the creed will not rule out of the enquiry as a disqualified witness. He shall be a man who is convinced that strict definition of doctrine is a right ideal, and also who is not repugnant to that severe statement of the eternal issues of faith and unfaith which certain clauses of that creed will put into his mouth. Let us follow such a man's experience as he reads and hears read this formulary.

'Whosoever will be saved, before all things it is necessary that he hold the Catholic faith, which faith except every man do keep whole and undefiled without doubt he shall perish everlastingly.' Our worshipper assents. He has correctly retranslated *vult salvus esse* into 'wishes to be saved'; has limited the reference of the creed to persons to whom the faith has been adequately presented; and he remembers that to 'perish everlastingly' must mean to 'lose that life which is of the eternal world.' So he assents.

But there follows 'And the Catholic faith is this...,' upon which there opens before his eye the long vista of metaphysical definitions, forty verses of statements about the laws of God's Being, of His relations to the Being of Man; that the Godhead is both One and Three, that the Three are uncreate, eternal, almighty, infinite, God, and Lord, but with the differences of a Son who is begotten, a Spirit who proceeds, that Jesus Christ is perfect God and perfect Man, yet not two but one Christ, that He has redeemed men and will judge them.

The prospect causes him shock. It is not because the words are the language of philosophy and hard for the plain man. He is no doubt bidden wander in what to himself is an austere wilderness, but he will traverse it, for in such austereness has God of old made the revelation of Himself. What has shaken him is not this, but the assertion that the Catholic Faith, *the faith which saves*, is *this*—the long array of metaphysical definitions. 'How can that be?' he murmurs.

'How can these things save a soul, or, if missed, cause the loss of it? These sentences of mortal speech, these fragmentary images of divine fact caught on the dusky mirror of human intelligence, these echoes of truth about the Godhead fallen from afar on the nerve of man's logical faculty, and that nerve only, while all else in the man, heart, conscience, will, may remain blind, deaf, unresponsive, impassible,—can it be that these sentences, or any that language can mould, *are* the Catholic Faith, are the equivalent of the ghostly force by which a man's soul is saved?' So he asks : and the heart which makes the theologian, and the reason which makes the reasoner, answers him No.

But already he has passed the point of shock : he finds himself reciting the Divine Attributes as man has gathered them from the inspired Book. He goes on this road, once entered, without a stumble. Some of the language is archaic, but then the Church too is ancient : obscure, but the unlearned may leave it to the learned : some appears to him to outrun the word of Scripture, but the Church, not he, is interpreter. His mind and will run on through the two score verses, along a road often rugged, but nowhere impassable, till at last it narrows in the grim defile of Judgement upon works good and evil. Here he walks through a valley of the shadow of death, but the rod and staff of the Divine Shepherd do comfort him, for he knows that the ' everlasting fire,' whatever thing it be, is an ordinance of a God whose nature

THE CHURCH PARTICULAR   161

is love, since only from His lips do we know the name of it. But then——.

'This is the Catholic Faith : which except a man believe faithfully he cannot be saved.'

'Then comes my fit again,' he cries. Here is the *impasse* across which his foot cannot travel. 'These forty verses, forty save one[1] pronouncements in metaphysic, however scriptural a metaphysic, are these the Catholic Faith, and can I not be saved except by believing these? Nay, can I by believing them be saved? What, shall the friend here worshipping at my side, the comrade of my chambers, a better man than I, if to be more selfless, truthful, brave is to be better, shall he, because he does not repeat with me the 'He rose from the dead,' since like Thomas, one of the Twelve, he thinks the physical wonder is attested by witness that has not been sifted as it needs, shall this man perish everlastingly?' And one worshipper's voice at this last verse drops from the chorus.

Why? What has happened to him?

This. He has been first required to affirm that man is saved by holding the Catholic Faith. He affirms this, for he believes it is so. Then he is required to affirm that this aforesaid Catholic Faith consists of certain intellectual propositions. But that is not so : the faith that saves is not these.

Next he is bidden rehearse certain propositions in which the Christian brotherhood has uttered its conception of God's nature and action. He rehearses

[1] "Rose again the third day," is not metaphysical, but historical.

L

them: for they are, he judges, true. But now he must add that these propositions if believed can save him; if disbelieved can make him to perish. But that is not so. These things, however true and to be believed, cannot, he is sure, be the faith which saves a soul. It costs more to redeem a soul.

But now let these two members of the formulary, the credal portion and the warning clauses, be drawn apart, and he can affirm both. He can aver that the Catholic faith is that we worship the One God in Trinity, and Trinity in Unity. And he can also aver, provided it be done in no connection with the former avowal, that a man who desires salvation must hold the Catholic faith. Why can he not join the affirmations? Because in the latter case the Catholic faith means the faith which has power to save, and in the former means not this faith, but the creed which can instruct but cannot *save*. He is required, in fact, to say that faith and creed are one and the same thing: and they are not one; they are two.

Those who would repeal the Quicunque find fault mostly with its temper, the harshness, as they consider, of the warning clauses. To the student of the formulary who speaks here it seems that not the temper is wrong, but the logic. The logic, however, not of those who made it, but of us who in this age use it. Those who framed and accepted the formulary were not at fault in their logic, but in the assumptions on which their logical process rested. They thought— I will rather say, they thought themselves to think—

that to believe a creed is to hold the faith. Then all was consistent : the warning clauses did not clash with the credal. *We* know, though we sometimes speak as if we had forgotten it, that creed is not faith; but we have shrunk from amending an error which so reverend an antiquity has sanctioned. But if, when we are seeking the ground of authority for the determining of truth and practice, we judge that a greater than antiquity is here to arbitrate, even Life, which was and is and is to be, we ought not so to shrink. We do not well when we fear to put asunder those two whom not God but man has joined together, the doctrines of the Quicunque which are a creed, and the clauses which are not a creed, but, standing where they now stand, are the assertion that a creed and a creed only can save a soul.

IX

'If we judge that a greater than authority is here, even Life.' The word recalls us to our true concern, which is to enquire not what is the right treatment of a formulary or a rubric imposing it, but whether the principle that Catholicity consists in Life is a principle which can be used in practice. We are testing it over the question of the use of one of our Creeds, and are asking if it is possible to know whether that use ministers life to the user, and by inference to the Church. It is submitted that this is a fact which is capable of being known; that the specific effect upon the reciter is a phenomenon which can be observed and estimated : that a judgement can be formed as to whether the religious vitality of a believer is heightened or is lowered by the recitation. Not all our judgements will agree. Some will be convinced that the Quicunque, in its present form of two logical incompatibles joined in one, cannot be responded to by a believer's soul, because part of him, his 'reasonable soul' or mental faculty cannot concur in the response; they will conclude that it is no ministry of life to him. Others may rate this disability of the creed as a less evil than the disablement of church authority or of positive doctrine which they fear from any change. This is only to say that facts which are subject to observation are apt to be differently reported by different observers. We have not here to decide between conflicting readings of the facts we have been studying. Such a decision was not the scope of our immediate reasonings; and, whichever be the decision at which the church may arrive, our present enquiry will equally be furthered by the poignant illustration of it. If we have been able to make it appear that facts of this spiritual nature, facts of a vitality in men's souls ensuant upon the formulation of a creed, can be observed at all, our purpose has been served : it has been successfully reasoned that the life in church or churchman, which is the deeper name for Catholicity, is matter of fact which we can verify and measure.

VII

THE HISTORIC CHRIST

[May 21st, 1911]

" **And so the Word** had breath."

VII

THE HISTORIC CHRIST

JOHN XIV. 6.—"I am the way, and the truth, and the life."

OUR enquiry into the nature of Creed has been throughout its course an endeavour to establish a theory of how the truth of creeds can be tested. The theory is that we can know our creeds to be true by the life which results to the soul when it believes. We claim for this principle that it offers a new method of research into religious truth, a Novum Organum, as it were, for a science of spiritual fact. The claim has no presumption; for the 'new method' is, we maintain, an old method and the oldest. Man always believed this way and in no other way. Man's belief in God is no other thing than man's life unto God : to believe *is* to live, and it is nothing else.

This organ of research we have tested on an article of the Creed which is cardinal, the Resurrection. We must test it lastly on an article which is more than cardinal, the all-inclusive tenet, the Incarnation. Why do we believe the Son of God was made man? Is it because believing we have life?

I

Incarnation is a word used not with double meaning

but with double reference. There is the Eternal Incarnation of the Lamb slain before the foundation of the world, a process of union of divine and human, which is, if rightly understood, the process of the creation by which God makes the worlds through the Son, a process which is eternally actualised for every soul of man when Christ is found in us. And also there is the Temporal or Historic Incarnation, the event once in time of the appearance of Jesus. The two events are aspects of one same truth, but for our study we need to distinguish them.

To apply our method to the eternal or spiritual Incarnation will ask no patience of a listener. No tedious analysis, such as we had to put in exercise over the test of the Resurrection truth is here required. There is a shorter way.

A Greek painter, when art was young, called his friend to view a new picture. Before it hung a curtain, which the visitor was bidden draw aside that he might see the painting: he reached his hand, but could not draw the veil: for, behold, the curtain was the picture.

We desire by this apologue to say that the idea of Incarnation is one thing with the idea of Life as by us conceived. Incarnation is the penetration of human by divine and the taking of manhood into God. 'I in you and you in Me,' is a scriptural name for this. Life is the same; the creature giving self to the Creator, the Creator rendering Himself to the creature. There is therefore no need to test the doctrine of an Incarnation by applying our instrument, the doctrine of Life. We do not come to the knowledge of an Incarnation in the soul by knowing of a life received in the soul; the one knowledge is the other. To say that the soul has life is to say that God indwells it. We do not pass through the curtain to come at the picture: for behold the curtain is the picture.

II

It is however not this spiritual and eternal Incarnation for which proof, by our own or by any method, is demanded. It is the historic Incarnation, the union of the divine with the human nature in the person of a man, Jesus of Nazareth, who presents Himself at one point in time and space, which the Christian is challenged to prove. Can we take up this challenge with the weapon of our organum of research? Can we show that Jesus is God and Man by this proof, that believing it we have life?

What is the historic Incarnation; what is it to say that Jesus was God?

This is the question on which at this moment many are speaking, while the people are in expectation and all men are musing in their hearts concerning Jesus, whether He is the Christ. Is this hour of our Church burdened with a less heart-searching issue than was the hour of Arius and Athanasius? If I approach the problem with small reference to these studies and speculations, it is not because of isolation from them, but because obvious limits impose on a speaker this economy in the presenting of such thought as is his own.

We must for the time, with those speculations, also put aside our familiar Christologies and their definitions of Jesus as God and Man, yet not two but one Christ, uniting two Natures in one Person. To depart from the established language of theology will not be presumptuous. For that language is the coinage of metaphysicians, and we, when we go out to encounter a giant difficulty of faith, must needs put off us that armour of the kings of theologic thought : we cannot go with this, for we have not proved it : we must arm our hand with our own familiar rustic sling, a certain homely conception which has been hitherto our weapon of research. We will take with us the conception, Life. We have a trust that here too it may give us the victory.

Whenever human knowledge has become scholastic, it must be rescued by the Interrogation of Nature. And our theologies are not untouched by this much of scholasticism that to the unlearned they seem unreal, to be not things but names. Let us draw the simple man with us to interrogate nature : invite him to see not how the Christ is one Person in Two Natures, but how when Jesus who is called Christ was born in Bethlehem, there happened a fact with effects upon the world, which have passed on to this man's self and can be experienced by him to-day.

For the historic Incarnation does not mean only the train of domestic and political incidents which formed the career of the prophet from Nazareth in Galilee. That would be a past fact, which our method could not touch, and only the method of historians can put to a test. The fact to which we give the name of Jesus Christ is that past occurrence *and all the consequences* of which it is the only and the complete cause. Among these is that occurrence which to each believer is not past but present, his own birth of faith, which is the happening of the Incarnation to himself. As we know that a star is set in the depth of the sky, because the spark of light which falls on our retina is the end of a star-beam, and star and beam are one continuous undivided fact, and our experience can touch the distant star when it touches this off-shoot of it; so we shall know that God was incarnate in Jesus two thousand years ago if we shall find that God is in our soul to-day; and that this which happens to ourself can be traced back in unbroken line of precedence to the day of Jesus as its sole and whole cause.

III

But this can be done. Let a man question the thing which happened to him when his faith was born. He will need perhaps to go back to memory's most 'dewy dawn,' the moment when the friend who was in Christ before him, the mother if he was so happy, spoke to his childish ear of the Unseen Things. Her word was of a 'Father that is in heaven.' There rose in him an image of this Father; that is, he gave his child intelligence over to a reality beyond his world of sense, and there came (did there not?) a power upon his mind. But also she spoke as one who had an affection towards this Reality, who was actually feeling the love she named for this Father. Thereupon a movement of affection stirred in her hearer, that is, he gave his heart to God, and his heart received a warmth, became a more vivid organ of the soul. And yet again she did things in his sight or knowledge answerable to what she spoke, deeds of kindness, selflessness, courage, patience, truth. At this a purpose awoke in him; that is, he gave the child's will up to the Not-Self, by willing like his teacher to please not self but It. This was life unto God which began. And if it was life in him, then it was in his soul the act of Incarnation. In that incident of a nursery hearth there passed an act of the world-process: there was a creative moment; the awaking of the first pulsation of a child's heart, set a-beat to the rhythm of the Heart of All Things, was as the shock which out of the lap of eternal night shook a universe.

For is it not so? When we ask how this thing happens, that the activity of one soul that has life makes life start in a new soul, we find ourselves peering into the primal mystery of how Being came to be. The disclosure is not made to us. As thou knowest not how the bones do grow in the womb, so thou knowest not what is the way of the spirit. Even in this body of death, our flesh, the coming of life is untrackable. What have we discovered more than this, that if actual and living life of flesh touches dormant and potential life of flesh, there springs a new life? So is every one that is born of the Spirit. Character makes character, said a sage; and faith, say we, makes faith. The life of a spiritual being is, as we have analysed it, the state or relation of mutual self-surrender between a soul and its Maker: and, when a soul that is in this state comes into contact with another soul, this same relation stirs in that other. Even as on our hearths coal kindles from coal, the black from the glowing; as at touch of the light and heat, which is already the condition of the live ember, there springs in the dead substance beside it the like condition; so at the touch of living spirit comes alive a spirit. Ever since the day of Prometheus man has known that life is fire; and fire life is indeed, this way. And this way our parents of the spirit gave us the life that was already theirs; this way the fore-fathers gave that life to them; this way the first fathers of the Church, witnesses of the Resurrection and men of the Pentecost, gave it to those first ancestors of ours; and this way did Jesus of Nazareth in Galilee give the life to the men and women who heard Him teach, saw Him do acts of life before the Baptist's messengers, watched Him die upon a cross; then received upon their hearts the 'Behold, it is I Myself,' and knew that in this Jesus, the man they loved, who was dead and is alive again, there was come upon the earth the life which cannot die by death, but by sacrifice is made alive. Thus we to-day from our parents, they yesterday from theirs, these again from the Apostles, received the committed fire, and the Apostles from Jesus the Galilean.

IV

Jesus Himself—from whom did He receive this life?

We have traced the Incarnation-fact, as it is found in a Christian's experience, back to Jesus: have gone up the stream of the tradition of a life unto God to reach a fountain head, the thirty years in Syria. What is there beyond that fountain head? No other stream that fills it: only the unseen, unknown fountains of the great deep of transcendent Being. *Exit in mysterium.* The life in Jesus is origin of the life in men, but of the life in Jesus no origin can be discerned. He is the river head underived, the unbegun Beginner, the cause of all, Himself uncaused. We venture to put forth as the fact which, at least for our human understanding, constitutes the Divinity of the Person of Christ this fact,—that the life He communicated to men was a new thing, not in the world of mortal things till then, which came there by an act of creation.

For 'where wast thou, O man, when God laid this new foundation of the world: declare it if thou hast understanding. Who determined the measures thereof, if thou knowest, or who stretched line upon it? Whereupon of things human were the foundations of this house of life fastened, and who laid the cornerstone thereof, when this second time the morning stars sang together and all the sons of God shouted for joy,—because Man was born alive?'

No language lesser than this elating rhythm of the grand creation-hymn seemed fit to echo our sense of the mystery veiled by the name of Jesus of Nazareth, son of Mary. Jesus is God incarnate in human kind because His personality, whatever be its relations to God the Absolute as they are known and named in heaven, can be named and known in earth as an act of creation. God said, Let there be Man, truly and wholly in our image and likeness, Man having perfectly the life unto God: and there was—the Man Christ Jesus. The thirty years of Jesus are the second stroke of creative power: this new Adam is the Man from heaven. It is the Lord's doing and not Nature's; and it is marvellous in our eyes.

V

The Lord's doing and not Nature's. It is this that will be challenged, where the Divinity of Christ is disputed; for the disputant will contend that Jesus, though in a sense new and even unique as a personality, yet was a fruit of the human evolution. To answer this by a mere *obiter dictum* in our present argument is not possible: it would be like setting forth a *summa theologiae* in a parenthesis. We can only point to where we find the proof. It is in the history of Christendom. For this fact, the personality of Jesus, is not comprised in the record of the thirty years but in the record of these and all the years that flow from them. The thing that is original, underived, unaccountable, is a certain happening in the large experience of mankind, the rise and persistence of the Christian character, recognisably in the Church, but discernibly also in the world. It is this happening which we call the Lord's doing and marvellous. It is provable, though not to prove in this place.

Yet to some of us who the most earnestly contend for the divinity of Jesus, may we not say that this Underivedness is the truth for which they are really contending, when they champion certain articles of our creed which are of value only as the historical correlatives of that truth, or as symbols of it. Thus, they assert the Virgin Birth of Jesus, as if the Divinity of Christ stood or fell with that physical event. It is not so—the manner of the Birth can have efficacy for human fate only as a fleshly accompaniment of the spiritual event, the entry into the human current of a force not derived from humanity. This entry is what we have to prove. This ought we to do, and not indeed to leave the other undone, but still to assure our hearts that, proven or found incapable of proof or disproof, it cannot shake our faith that God sent forth His Son; sent Him forth made of a woman; but His Son. Sometimes now we fight for a symbol when we should fight for the substance; as ere now in campaigns of our countrymen, a regiment has lost a victory by a useless strife to save the colours. Are not we liable to do the same—to remember the banner, forget the battle?

Yet when we assert the underivedness of the life that was in Jesus, the immediacy of the Creator's action in the making of it, we do not deny the evolution in Him of human elements. On the contrary a Christian lays much stress on the signs of a preparation for the Christ, of a fulness of time when God sent forth His Son. But the constituents out of which issued the life in Christ were elements in some measure of earth, but in an over-proportion beyond all measure were elements of heaven. Those human and natural antecedents do not in all their sum make up the sum of the constituents which built up that Reality: they are indeed no more the cause of Jesus than the molecules of his corporal frame, with the mechanical and chemical forces which combined them, were the cause of His living body of flesh. As that body which was made of earth's dust and her mechanism and chemistry was, not a man, but some of the makings of a man, till the breath of life was breathed into the nostrils, so into the thin stream of nature's evolution of manhood entered—Jesus. On that instant the slender current became a march of waters, with volume, breadth, momentum, as if through a floodgate of the Unseen had been poured from fountains of the great deep the river of all the water of life.

VI

Have we, in this conception of the historic Incarnation as a fresh creative act of God, taken flight back again from our proposed interrogation of nature to the metaphysic of church doctors, who have always described the Redemption as a 'new creation'?

We are back again no doubt in metaphysics, but it is an interrogation of nature that has brought us there. The sound path which our research into fact has footed has carried us through nature's territory till we came to that precipice edge where the border of the finite marches with the infinite, a brink beyond which not the foot but the wing must voyage. All interrogations of nature lead to that brink. Trace back the physical life on our planet through all its generations, and you reach a seed dropped on earth, as physicists have surmised, from 'moss-grown fragments,' the wrecks of an earlier world, itself peopled with seeds of living things from who knows what yet older world. Or if life should after all discover its parentage in the chemical and mechanical nature, whence was begotten the primal ether which came to be woven on the looms of that mechanism and chemistry? There is still that leap of Being out of the dark. Or trace back the spiritual in man, as the artist's 'creations,' and the line of intellectual descent can be followed no further back than to the poet 'waiting for the spark from heaven to fall.' Or unravel the evolution of a Paul from Pharisee to

Apostle, and the thread breaks at the point of a conversion which is 'wonderful': you cannot see the bridge of process across which the Incarnate One has entered the saint: 'it *pleased God* to reveal His Son in Him'; there is no more to say.

To this brink of the gulf then we are brought when we track the life of Christian faith backward to the appearance in history of Jesus, who transmits a life which no one had transmitted to Him. Observation of fact serves us no longer: another faculty must here pursue the interrogations. It is the Imagination, claimed earlier by us as thought's greater instrument: it is the study of facts with the soul's spiritual posture of Wonder, according to that reported saying of Jesus 'Wonder at that which is before you.'

Wonder, we repeat, is the response of a soul to the new which is also great. It is the Virgin asking 'How shall this be?' yet answering, Be it unto me. By Imagination wondering we open our soul to the inflow of a world of spiritual fact for which the vessel of our merely sensuous experience is not deep enough and its channel too strait. By this energy the soul becomes her own organ of knowledge: she makes assay of the eternal reality behind the temporal by the life which she experiences or fails to experience when with that reality she makes the contact, called believing, which is the intercommunion of the Finite and the Infinite.

We have now defined by our inductive enquiry (which led us at last up to this brink of mystery) the fact which we are to test by our method—the historic Incarnation.

VII

To believe in this fact is to believe that a Christian's personal experience of a life unto God in him has for its first cause the event called the doings and sufferings of Jesus of Nazareth. This belief—that a historical personage is the cause of our spiritual life—is to be subjected to proof by our method. When our soul believes in the historic Christ, believes, that is, that all which Jesus did between the first at Bethlehem and the last on Olivet, is the ultimate origin in human history of her salvation; briefly, when the soul has faith in the person of Christ Jesus, divine and human, does she have life?

There is a great division of this proof which need not be laboured. To array the evidence that men's hearts and wills have been vivified by a devotion to Jesus as a Divine Person; to muster the testimonies of churches given in creed or deed, to cite the utterances of saints who confess the story of Jesus to be the source of their energies and affections—this might seem a needless pomp of rhetoric. It is so certain that the power upon a Christian's purpose and emotion has been the power that has gone out from the personality which he touches through the record. From Peter, who believed that Jesus was Lord and Christ, because God had raised Him up, and Paul (too hastily marked for their own by idealist interpreters as 'knowing Christ no more after the flesh') whose spiritual wrestle and victory it was to strive and not prevail against the Man whom Stephen declared—from these captains of our faith it is all one story onward to the village enthusiast of to-day who tells you that he 'does not care much now for what folks call enjoyments, but what I like to do, when I have any time to myself, is to get into some old cupboard or behind a heap of straw in the stable, and pour out my soul to the Lord Jesus'; and as he speaks there falls a beam upon the homely features and lights up to you the honesty within. It is this Lord Jesus, the Christ not of metaphysic but of history, who has been for this man's heart and will the power of God unto salvation.

Yet since things seen are mightier than things heard, and our own experience outweighs all report of others, let a believer ask himself whether in those approaches to the Divine which most are mystical and where most he is 'in the Spirit,' it is not the story of a Man which strongliest animates his power to will. He has come to the Sacrament which shows the Lord's death in history, before an hour of hazard or decision, of encounter or suffering, that he may eat the bread of comfort and drink the cup of holy Passion. There before the altar

> "As a man calls for wine before he fights,
> Or asks one draught of earlier, happier sights,
> Ere fitly he can hope to play his part,"

even so this worshipper knows that the force which

there enters him comes by a devotion which is a remembrance of 'earlier sights,' remembrance of one Man and His deed in story, how in the days of His flesh He endured a mortal's agony, and in no ideal but most actual Passion gave his members to a death which brake a mortal body and poured the life-blood. Let this worshipper be witness to himself whether heart was warmed and will was sinewed by an event, that once on a time and on one spot of earth befell one man, Jesus the Galilean. It will be his witness whether the belief in a historic Christ makes life in the soul.

VIII

But we hasten on to the proof more demanded of us. The historical critic of our faith may grant us the quickening of heart and will by a Christ of story; though he will say the believer has mistaken that animation's cause, which is not an event but the impulsion only of an idea, to which the Christ-tale serves as helpful symbol. With our mind, he will say, it is otherwise. An idea which has crystallised into a relation to an imagined Person—this a Christian can perhaps love and obey: what he cannot do is to think it. His intelligence does not live by a surrender to this belief: on the contrary it refuses to believe in a Jesus who is a Christ. Thought faints and is annulled in an effort to assimilate this idea. It cannot salute, as the presence of the Divine in humanity, an individual man at one epoch of time, and an individual too who had so little claim to a universal significance as this Jewish preacher, this person who however good was a personality of one kind only, a man of one trade and a humble one, a carpenter; one whose mind had the limitation of a narrow peasant ignorance; whose character offers to some critics' judgement even a blemish here and there, such as an inadequate sensitiveness to social injustice done to wife or slave; and whose fanatic temperament could prophesy for his cause an apocalyptic victory, which did not happen, and force on a martyrdom, which for an illumined conscience is a wrongful self-immolation, to be repented of on the cross.

This allegation, that a historic Incarnate One can be loved and obeyed but cannot be thought; that, if heart and will can live unto such a Christ, yet the intelligence cannot so live, must be met. And met on its own ground and terms, not evaded, as has too often been the strategy of apologetics, by disparaging the value of the understanding in the activity, faith.

That forlorn scholar of the 17th century, Vincent Flaccius, who had fought his sicknesses with a life-power he found in a scholar's activities, bade grave on his tombstone the testimony, '*Vita sine literis somnus, sine Christo mors est.*' And we say after him that our life, if without Christ it is but death, even with Christ, but without intelligence, is a life not dead indeed but much asleep; Christ is come to awake it out of sleep. My mind must live unto Christ made man, my mind with all else that is within me. 'I will live with the spirit,' we exclaim as might Paul; 'I will live with the understanding also.'

Can we then live with the understanding also unto this truth, that the Man Jesus was God's Incarnation in history?

IX

The critics urge that, if emotion and energy can thrive on the acceptance of a historic Christ, thought on the other hand languishes in the effort and dies. We must look into this. What thought is it which encounters this deadening repulse? Perhaps it is a thought concerning Jesus which is unreal and ought to die. Is it a thought of Jesus, the individual, as identical with the Absolute?—an idea certainly unthinkable. Of Jesus as the Teacher who reveals the nature of God, or as the full and perfect exemplar of all varieties of human conduct?—ideas which the mental limitations and the brief, narrow moral experience of a Jewish craftsman seem to forbid. Of Jesus as the consummator of man's evolution?—an idea which His momentary and solitary position, midway in the secular process, makes incredible to evolutionary science. Or is the thought of Jesus of a kind that undergoes shock, when it is met by that speculative reading of His ministry which would present him to us as the dupe of an apocalyptic fantasy, and the victim of a wilfully self-inflicted doom? Here no doubt are difficulties under which the faith of many withers as by a frost. We would invite them to think more largely of the office of the Christ, and to note how vital warmth returns. Jesus has been to them the Teacher and Revealer of truths, or the Example and the Guide of conduct. These He is, but these are not He. These are aspects of His deed, facets of His being, beams which ray out from His glory, not the glory, the being, the deed. We seek the Jesus behind all these and within them all, that which He is first and last and midmost.

X

We believe that we have found it when we recognise in Jesus not the divine Teacher, divine Exemplar, but the divine LIFE. He came as man not that we might be instructed, exampled, disciplined, but that we might have life and have it abundantly. He is Way and Truth and Life. The Truth, for by Him we know the world-secret, what God and Man is: the Way, for His footsteps trace the believer's walk: but first and midst and last he is the Life; the Life which is the light on men's path, the Life which is their strength to walk therein. His birth in the flesh was the Creator's second stroke, that struck into man, already become a living soul, the power to live indeed, by living not unto his world but unto his God. See if to think of Jesus as the Life does not wither at their root the doubts that were withering our faith. Did we doubt if Jesus was God Incarnate because we could not find the Absolute within the bounds of this one human personality? No, for the Absolute is not there : but is Life not there? In the act of Jesus, in the patience and the venture and the sacrifice of self which lost life only to find it, we do discern a personality which was human and yet lived wholly unto God. Did we doubt that Jesus, being one man and at one moment out of all time, and contravening the law of continuous and gradual evolution, could be of a universal significance? But Jesus was a Life; and life, though it can evolve when once it has come into being, must first come to be; and that beginning can only be by a creative stroke, must happen at some one point in time and by the passage at a leap from the moment of 'There was not' to the moment of 'God said let there be, and there was life.' An evolution of the Christ there was and is, in Christian history, continuous surely and surely gradual enough to fulfil all rightness of evolution's law. But first it needed to begin : and this beginning Jesus was. And life, if there was to take place life in humanity, could not be otherwise than in one man. It could not be in less than a man, for life is the living unto God of a human nature, not of a nature's part. It needed not to be in more than one : for if one man were alive unto God, the fire of life was already kindled, and all the dead could kindle at it. Did we doubt how a carpenter of Nazareth, a humble provincial in the kingdom of all time and all existence, could comprehend in his narrow self the immensity of human thought and human character,

THE HISTORIC CHRIST 187

and be the recapitulation of human kind? But Jesus was not man's thought or character: He was man's life. He was in germ the union of God with man, He was the Surrender of human spirit to divine Spirit. But this Surrender and Union could be realised in any nature and career and experience, however limited or however enlarged. There needed only that a Self should be given to God. Were it self of wide experience or self of narrow, mattered not; it mattered only that the Self was given and was given wholly. Is the sacrifice of a king, who offers his life in battle, more a sacrifice on his own part than is the offering of his humblest follower? Each offers all that he has, his Being: they are equal in their deed. The Self then of the Galilean working man was oblation rich enough: it was a whole burnt-offering; the fire of the Lord fell on it: and when it flamed, life was kindled in the earth.

XI

Last, have we doubted if Jesus were indeed the man from heaven, because He predicted a coming on the clouds to judgement, and because He did the actions and spoke the words which entailed a death He clearly foresaw, and could have avoided, but of set purpose provoked? Why, let this reading of the story be granted to the full, and then ask yourself whether by that reading Jesus becomes any less the Life. Yield the critic his contention, (on which scholarship must finally pronounce), that Jesus did verily believe in His near return with apocalyptic wonders. You have only yielded that Jesus was a man of a generation which had in the minds of its more spiritual members imaged its faith in the victory of Good over Evil in this picture of a material and proximate event; that He presented to His own faith that victory in those conceptions which, unless a miracle were done upon His mind, were the only mode in which His faith could utter itself. When He so pictured His return upon the clouds, it was a dream, if you will, but a dream by which He lived unto God. It was the very force and livingness of His faith which enabled Him to see that vision : the Parousia He pictured was the translation of that lively faith into a mortal language; it was material because it was so real, it was near because it was so sure.

Let us make this reasoning human by an apologue, Joan the Maid in prison hearing from her Voices that she shall be rescued 'by a great deliverance.' How did she picture it? A rally doubtless of her countrymen, or a baring of the sword of Michael. The deliverance came, but so as by fire : and through the fire came her confession ' my voices have not deceived me.'

Yield the critic again that far more precarious and arbitrary speculation of a self-immolation, and still the perfectness of the character of Jesus stands untouched. For 'ought not Christ to have suffered this thing?' It did behove the Messiah to press to clear and undeniable decision the Messianic issue, the quarrel of Heaven and the World. How else then but by this implacable self-assertion, demanding from Israel, in heaven's name, not something, not much, but all? The battle must be plainly set and visibly fought out and won. The end could be foreseen, could be averted? Yes, as the soldier stepping to the front for a forlorn hope can foresee a death under the rampart, and can, if he will, stay back in the ranks. What should Jesus have done, by this critic's counsel? When Jerusalem's front hardened and threatened, doubtless it behoved the Christ to steal back in peace to friendly Galilee, and there tell them once more that he who loseth his life shall find it. How?—when the life has *not* been found nor lost. Who believes then this preacher's report? to whom has the arm of the Lord been revealed through this gentle provincial moralist, who is in word but not in power? But to dally with surmises of what might have been—how petty it is in us, who can know not what *might* have been, but what *was*! That self-immolation stands approved as rightful by the answer from heaven. The deed of self-assertion unto death did prosper, the sacrifice did work salvation; a Christian can live to-day the believer's life unto God, *because* Jesus defied the priesthood, perished by their hands, and by the rising from the dead brought to light immortality, the life that is born from the travail of life's surrender.

"Ah! but," some critic insists, "you may explain away the apocalyptic hope, but not the despair of an apocalypse. Besides the 'Ye shall see the Son of

Man coming in the clouds,' there is also the 'My God, why hast thou forsaken me.' Interpret the first to be an act of life, and still the second is a confession of death.''

Surely of the Passion which makes Life that despair was the last and all-completing moment : achievement could not forego it. This also it behoved the Christ to suffer, this last detachment from self, to surrender wholly the hope of a way of escape : this (dare we say it in words reputed to be a precept of His?) was 'the wondering of Jesus at that which was before Him,' the utter opening of His soul to the unimaginable in the counsels of God that passed all understanding, the last gasp of wonderment that the Father should ask of His Son even this, that He consent to be forsaken!

There are gentler interpretations of the cry on the cross, as that Jesus was but citing from the psalm an ancient agony like to His. We choose the severer. Jesus did undergo the moment of despair, despair of deliverance. Here was the full up-render of self, which made the burnt-offering whole. By the utterance in which hope's last harp-string broke, the Redeemer for us men and our salvation died the death into life eternal.

XII

Is this enough to say? Are we content with proving that in a historic Christ, as well as in a mystical, the mind *can* believe? We rise from a duly patient study of alleged difficulties of belief to assert that a Christian fully believes in a mystical incarnation only when he believes in a historic.

'If two of you shall agree on earth as touching anything that they shall ask, it shall be done for them,' said the Christ. Why should the prayer of two prevail? Because the force of prayer has become twofold? No, the prayer is not multiplied; it is transmuted. My act of faith while it is solitary, remains, in the dry technicality, a merely subjective belief, and therefore an uncertain. Let me see that belief also in another man, and it has become objective and therefore real. As I make myself sure of a world of things external to myself by the touch of my hand on it, so I make sure that the spiritual world is real by touching this reality in that which is outside myself, this other man. The experience which was inward, now is outward: it has become part of a world which is objective. But next, the belief, verified already as soon as I find it anywhere at all in the Other than Self, is confirmed when I find it not in one point of the Other but in many points; not in the one or two, but in the multitude of them that believe, the Church Catholic and Apostolic, that is, the Body of Christ that is everywhere and in all times. And still full assurance tarries. For the Church Catholic is not actually all men, is universal in idea but not yet in fact. May not this belief in an Incarnation be a subjective fancy, though not of one but of many? Ah! too easily. But—'see the Christ stand'! That Incarnation which I have felt within my separate self, which I have experienced in the two or three, which I have discerned in a vast section of my kind—lo! I have seen it not in the few, not in the many, but in All. For I have seen it in this Jesus of history, the One who is the Whole, the Individual who is also the Universal, the perfect, all-comprehending manhood; Jesus, who though he was not all men, yet was all of man. In Him, this all of man, I experience the Incarnation; in Him I behold effected the union of earth and heaven, finite and infinite, mortal and eternal: for in this one man and one event I behold a Life that lives unto God indeed. The timid faith that is in my bosom has ventured out, has reached thither her questioning finger, reached thither her mistrustful hand, has touched and proved an Incarnation which is substance and reality in the Other than Self, in the solid world of things that are. By Jesus Christ born of woman the mystic union of the soul and her Maker has become a thing which our eyes have seen and our ears heard and our hands have handled. An Incarnation which is there in history is an Incarnation which is there in verity. God has made this Jesus whom a woman bore and men slew on a cross to be the outward visible pledge of man's inward and spiritual birth unto life divine; has instituted in Him a Sacrament that enables faith.

XIII

Without a parable spake He not unto them—the Son of God in the days of His flesh. Without a parable of Sacrament speaks not to us the Father of spirits.

What weight upon the human will lies in the force among things we name Sacrament, none need here asseverate. All that weight upon whosoever wills to be saved lies in the event of time, which laid bare to our senses the timeless process of creature's reconcilement to Creator. Since One Man wrought in Galilee and died at Zion, the soul of man naturally Christian and groping after God if haply it might find Him, has had the Whither of its quest beaconed to the eye, has had signalled to the ear the Way thereto and the When. 'Behold, the Cross of Jesus, that is the goal : behold, Love's sacrifice on it, that is the way : and now, even when thou art beholding, now is the accepted time.' And thereupon the lonely mortal will, that does not dare make choice, but hangs yet in the wind, faltering and unresolved, has caught the mighty rhythm of the power of Sacrifice, where it pulses through the boundless All; has timed by it the stroke of spirit which seals a fate; has made by venturousness the great acceptance, of the Passion which is the Life of man.

VIII

CREED AS SACRIFICE, AN APPEAL

[May 28th, 1911]

"Our wills are ours, to make them Thine"

VIII

CREED AS SACRIFICE, AN APPEAL

Is. LVII. 19.—"Peace, peace, to him that is far off, and to him that is near, saith the Lord , and I will heal him."

ON this last opportunity under the statute of this lectureship, the attempt must be made to gather into one focus the trains of reflection on the nature and function of Creed which have occupied us throughout.

Creed is an instrument of man's salvation. But salvation is best figured, at least for our own day, under the image of Life, the highest expression yet attained of the fact of existence. Life, studied in all its kinds and degrees, proves to be the mutual self-upgiving of organism and environment, of creature and Creator. Creed then can be an instrument of life only by enabling this interchange of self. This it does by enabling the creature to render its own part in that mutual action. When a believer recites a creed, either he does nothing at all, or he offers by help of the words a sacrifice to the Creator of his whole personality, thought, emotion, conduct together. Of the three elements in confession, the mental has no doubt a prominence to our consciousness in a creed which is verbal, though in a creed which should be not in word but in the form of worship or of code of conduct (and each is a creed), the prominence would be with the emotional or the practical element. But the mental element cannot exist in abstraction, nor can it be understood except as in union with the others. The forgetting of this has caused much confusion in theology, and some disablement in religion.

Creed then is, we judge, an indispensable means of effecting a soul's self-surrender to reality. By recital of a formula a man can utter his faith, make it outward, objectify it, discover and contemplate it in the other than self. By the utterance he makes a self-committal to a way of thinking, a course of conduct, a bestowal of the affections. Thus Creed is the instrument of salvation by enabling the believer's act of self-surrender which is half the act of life. If the Divine makes response by giving itself to the man; if the man's thought is answered by illumination, his affection by a love shed abroad in his heart, his energy by an invigoration that falls on his will, then the reciprocation has happened, and the man has life. But this life resultant from confession of a creed is the truth of creed; the man has believed aright.

Creed ministers life to us. But that can only be if creed is itself alive; or, to speak more exactly, if it is such that he who recites it can be alive in the act of recital. Creed is alive when the echo of its phrases starts a movement of the soul in the hearer, as of old a music could start an inspiration in a prophet. If the phrases should be without meaning for him, and even without those associations by which mere sound can arouse, as a music does, a movement of the spirit; still more if the meaning contradicts his other beliefs; then the creed in that part of it does not minister life. All language of mortals is 'a body of death,' and the creeds are language of mortals, and able like it to die.

I

If these positions are made good, what follows that concerns our faith and practice? Are we to believe and to do any otherwise than as we have all the centuries believed and done?

Some Christians, one observes, think that very much needs doing. They plead that the existing language of the two longer creeds is that of a superseded metaphysic, and where not out of date is out of the comprehension of most worshippers; that there are articles even in the simplest formulary which are no longer held true in their original sense, and at least one article the historic validity of which some of the faithful cannot affirm with the old absolute assurance; that in consequence the use of the creeds in public worship is an inconvenience, or even for some consciences a mischief; and that it would be well to discontinue their use.

The plea should be met neither with anger nor even with disrespect. These protesters against creed are still entangled in the error that faith is of the mind, and that creed helps faith by its work upon the intelligence. But it is the soul to which creed has to minister; and it ministers by words which best can stir the life-movement in that soul towards union with the divine realities symbolised. Those words must be ancient words, carrying the continuity and catholicity of the church, if they are to carry the spell of a communion with a faith which was and is to be. Their fixity has inconvenience: their mutability would have mischief. What unthrift it would be to exchange the power on heart and will, which flows out in the echo of the catholic watchwords, for some small gain of appeal to the intelligence. A gain too so easily recoverable. For as in the secular commonwealth we re-adjust the misfits worked in its statutes through time and change by the instrument of equity which re-interprets letter by spirit, or by silent abrogation of a letter that is dead; so the laws of the spiritual commonwealth can be re-vitalised, if need call for it, by the consent, tacit or overt, of clerus and populus to let the symbol stand indeed unchanged, but stand for a new and better apprehension of the truth.

This indeed is what the Church is doing. We teach our catechumens that the resurrection of the body means a real resurrection of the person; and we let them understand that the Procession from the Son, momentous to the Churches as the article has been in history, is in the salvation of a soul of lesser moment, if of any moment at all.

This then is a conclusion as to practice which the

Church has already drawn from the premise held by her, somewhat too inarticulately, that creed is to minister not a knowledge but a life. The practice of reinterpreting a creed in any member of it which has suffered the touch of mortality, from which no speech of man is immune, is a catholic practice; it need stir no alarm or scruple in those who have the catholic mind. In practice then we see not much that is to be done, other than what the Church does already—except indeed (but that is a great matter) to do it openly, avowedly, without shame of face or inward misgiving; to do it not, as usual, belatedly and as a concession to expediency, but timely and as the exigence of our principles, a fruit and consequence of a lively faith.

II

But when we turn from practice to faith, it will appear there is much to be done, and very much. There is for very many of us certainly a new posture of mind to be taken, perhaps even a conversion in our thinking to be undergone. When we have recognised that faith is a soul's surrender to a Divine which renders itself in answer; that creed is an instrument to enable this surrender; that the verbal creed enables specifically the surrender of the reasoning soul, and has no other use or worth but this: do we thereupon recognise what call to sacrifice has been prepared for us by our principle? It is a call to make ready a sacrifice for the altar, a sacrifice of our thoughts; thoughts that are our self, being our own now, however once they were received from that which is not ourself.

For what has been the thought about our creeds which has been the predominating and characterising thought of those in our English church who for more than half a century by the force alike of their piety and their scholarship have determined the faith-movement of their church? It is the thought which centres itself in the categories of a Revelation, a Deposit, a Tradition. A Revelation by which a knowledge of unseen realities was communicated to man's mind; a Deposit of doctrines interpreting that knowledge; a Tradition, by the articles of formularies and the lessons of authorised doctors, of the good thing once for all committed to the saints. This thought of Churchmen how was it attained? It was attained by a Passion. Who reads that Oxford story and the story of a church into which it swelled, and does not know that the names of those who revived the dimmed vision and torpid activities of the Anglican communion are names of men who were, in that ancient phrase, 'a company of the white martyrdom,' a company of those 'who for the love of God sever themselves from all they love though they suffer privation ('fasting') or trouble thereby:' men, whom the facts of their time did not call to resist unto blood, but who for the love of Christ forsook self that they might live by the holiest truth their souls could reach, in scorn of consequence.

CREED AS SACRIFICE, AN APPEAL

These men, our fathers, found and held their creed by a Passion. To us by a tradition they committed that good thing. We to-day then—by a Passion we must hold it, by a sacrifice of self we must maintain it. Do we discern what that sacrifice has to be? For it may be a sacrifice of any of our thoughts about our creeds: may be the offer to surrender that central tenet, that creeds once fashioned by the early undivided church can never more be changed; that the Church has but one duty towards them, to keep undiminished the treasure of a revelation committed to her, coined in the language of the primitive symbols of belief; that she is the witness of

"Christes lore and His apostles twelve,"

and must guard uncorrupt the letter of that lore against any who would alter, add, diminish.

And so might it have been, if Christes lore had been a lore; had it been a thing learned, that could be framed in the letter of a creed; had the matter of the tradition been a code of conduct, a table of articles, a record of events; had it been a treasure we are to keep safe, and not a fire we are to keep alight. But Christ's lore is not a letter but a life. Christ is not, first and last, Revealer, or Teacher, Exemplar, Guide. He is the Way, the Truth, and the Life, but He is Way and Truth because He is the Life. The good thing He has committed to us is not a doctrine for the mind nor a rule for the will: is not a word but a power; the ineffable power by which when God said 'Let there be' behold, there was; is the current of creative energy issuing from the act of Jesus in time and space, and passing through earth's dust always and everywhere to quicken it into living souls of men: it is the divine spark in the soul, of which the mystic dreams, the 'something in our embers that doth live,' the holy fire which Christ said He came to send on earth; yea, the fire of the divine-human sacrifice, the sacrifice of reconciliation, the Love which seeks and saves, the passion which redeems by making live, the eternal passion that is the gravitation on which the universe is built, the magnet on which it is strung; a force that vibrates for ever across the infinite plasmic ether out of which the worlds are woven, thrilling into flame the spirits here and there of the great ones—prophet, priest, confessor, martyr —who shine as beacon lights in the world, and touching into trembling glow a thousand times ten thousand taper points of that multitude whom no man can number, the good who are not great.

III

This evermoving flame of Sacrifice, this life-breath of an eternal Passion that makes things to live —this is the good thing committed to us, and our tradition is to convey this. But a passion we cannot convey except by passioning: the altar can burn with a perpetual sacrifice only by a burnt offering daily laid on it. We do not lay on the altar the daily offering of our thought when we say 'Thus have I thought out, or thus have I received as thought out by

my fathers in Christ, the interpretation of the truths which God spake in times past by His Christ and the prophets of Christ: and thus, no otherwise, will I judge the truth and word it, until the Lord come.'
What change in our words of creed, or whether any at all, will be required of us; whether our sacrifice will go on to consummation, or be arrested, we cannot know; but of a surety we cannot bargain this. Though it were the first-born of our soul, though it carried all the divine promise to us, we must bind our first-born to the horns of the altar, and take the knife to slay the victim, until there cries out of heaven 'Lay not thine hand upon it; neither do thou anything to it: for now I know that thou fearest God, seeing thou hast not withheld thy son, thine only son, from me.'

Is there need to state this in colder formal language for clearness sake? What is here pleaded for is not a practical action but a spiritual disposition. But this is a disposition vital to faith. To attain it may be a conversion that saves. The Creed we should safeguard without re-verifying might be in all ways right in itself, but it would not be right for us. Indeed we cannot safeguard so even the Letter of it: for that Letter has no value or reality, it becomes a nothing in the world, that moment when we profess it no longer in the spirit of sacrificer.

IV

Let us not turn the edge of the claim on us to make our creed-holding a passion, by telling ourselves that already there is essential sacrifice in that submission of the individual's religious predilections to a Catholic standard, which the Church urges on the churchman, or that it is others rather than ourselves who in belief refuse the sacrificer's attitude; as the protester of the indefeasible private judgement, who refuses the catholic surrender of the self-sufficiency of conscience; or as the reasoner upon truth who refuses the surrender of reason's self-sufficiency, reproaching us the while for disloyalty to truth, because he fails to see what truth is, and thinks that truth is logic. We will not ask 'Lord, and what shall these men do?' We will follow the Lord, to a Passion. And if we are satisfied that already we are doing this, for that our faithfulness to the unchanged 'deposit' of faith is a real sacrifice, we will remember that even in faith the sacrifice of man, though it cost him much, is nought, unless it is answered by the fire of God; and that a confession is an answered sacrifice, a reciprocation with God, only if by it the confessor has life and life abundantly.

If the confessor has life. But life, the life in our thoughts, life which is the knowing of reality—what is it for the thinker in religion? Ask what it is for the thinker in any material. It is, we say, a relation of a Mind to Things, of Subject to Object. It is the Subject discovering itself in the objective world, the going forth of the subject and its return into itself. A naked diagram this of a bleak science, epistemology. Yet on that bare frame of the logician can be caught and held up to our studying eyes the glimpses, fugitive else, which disclose to us faith's realities. For the error of the too dogmatic believer and that of his opposite are but contrasted ways of exaggerating the one term or the other in that reciprocity of subject and object which makes the life of soul when it thinks. The dogmatist rests all proof on the historic—that is, the objective—element in belief, on the record of events, and the record of the church's interpretation of them. The anti-dogmatist rests all on the experiential element, the personal consciousness, the subject. Both miss the give and take between subject and object, the interdependence of the two factors by which thought has life. We do not know God with full assurance by the story of Jesus, and we do not know him by the experience of a Christ within the man. We know God by a history wed to an experience, by our bosom's sense of the Divine found reflected in the outer world of fact, by a story of all that Jesus began both to do and to teach found to repeat itself in things taught and done upon the believer's soul to-day. Let them cease recriminations, dogmatist and idealist, and learn one from the other what the faith of each must add to itself before it is a faith that lives indeed.

V

And may we not ask believers of catholic mind to consider another ground of the claim made by this our organ of faith, the principle of Life, to be an authority in religion by the side of their own authority of Tradition and History? This ground is its power to catholicise: the promise and potency in it of Christian unity. Observe that promise in the action of the principle within our own church of England. She is Christendom's best magnet to reunite the churches—unless and until we rend that unity by intolerances of the schools, or by some impatient policy of change in her national status set free the forces of disruption which her oneness now restrains. Observe, I pray you, how Life as a ground of authority is a bond that draws our differences together. For this is the All-Truth that underlies the truths parcelled out to each. Life, the life of wholeness and corporateness, is (we trust that we showed this earlier) the catholicity of the catholic believer. Life, the life of individual and immediate intercourse with God, is the experiential religion of the evangelical Christian. Life, the life of the free Spirit, the life of growth, freedom, change, re-adaptation, is the liberty of prophesying asserted by the champion of rationality. What each holds of sound doctrine is but a translation of some one potency of the mystic life, and because and while they have hold on life, they are holden each in the unity of the one spirit. Life is the church's magnetic centre. No magnet of Tradition, no doctrine, formula, ritual, order, discipline, or use can draw her many into one, except as itself has been magnetised of life.

Does there not at this moment offer itself a test of the value of life as an eirenicon in churchmen's differences? We are in difference about a rubric, whether the plainness or the richness of the symbolic dress in which we outwardly clothe our chief mystery is the right interpretation of the church's rule. That an agreement will be reached by the ways of legal or historical scholarship seems hardly to be hoped. Let us submit the question to the test of life. We shall do so, if we grant liberty of option, and learn by experiment which system proves more to make vitality of soul in those who use it.

VI

If however it is ventured that this principle of Life can be an organ of faith, a test of truth, and a ground of authority in religion, side by side with the principle of the objective or historic and in an indissoluble interdependence on it, it is earnestly pleaded that what is ventured here is nothing new. To claim that it is new would indeed not be presumption only but self-condemnation, since in faith there can be nothing new. No 'new commandment' can be given, 'but an old one which we had from the beginning.' None the less let one to whom it has presented itself confess, that where it has risen upon the mind there has dawned a light of interpretation, which searches out all the wide fields of human belief and practice, an interpretation which sheds light abroad over their tangling perplexities, arresting doubts, twilight yearnings, in 'a largess universal, like the sun.'

VII

And yet, even yet, a word may be addressed to a most human instinct in minds among the most devout. They will feel that we invite them to move their foot from the 'impregnable rock' of a scripture, the letter of Tradition, and launch into a void, this intangible, mystical life-response of spirit. Who can trust the weight of his soul to a footing so precarious? But *is* life precarious? It may seem so. The marvel that the rhythm of the heart can in a thousand million beats encounter no jar to silence it! That at its side the breath keeps an unarrested even march when the most trivial violence might disorder all into ruin! But life, the precarious, is the most stable among things, stable in the very degree of its precariousness; the subtlest organisms and the most venturous are those which live with largest range and, by the measure not of clock-time but of action, with longest duration. Nor let our metaphor of the rock mislead us. Rock is not always a house's best foundation; it is the worst —in earthquake. Let us remember how for early symbolists the image to inspire was a thing of least fixity: it was a ship riding a storm, the Navicella of the Church, of all things the most unstable, yet by waves the least to be overthrown; for, like life, it masters nature by yielding, by obedience it makes the winds and the waves obey it, persists in being by true response to facts that be.

VIII

Our pleading of the cause of Creed, the Creed of the Christian, with such frail understanding and faltering interpretation as this pleader can bring to it, here must end, so far as it is addressed to those within the Church, to the people of the Creed.

There remains a brief word of pleading to them that are without, or who so account themselves; to those who reject the Christian's creed, perhaps not knowing what it is; to those who are the people of an alien creed, which they esteem a better, and a warring one; to those who have no creed at all, or who think that they have none.

Those who reject Christianity as a creed outworn, the educated abstainers from its worship, the men of the Defection. 'Your Creed' say they 'no longer tells the story of the world-process: it is a nursery tale for earth's babes, not her grown-up family. Tell the fairy story of 'once upon a time' to those who are children still: leave us with our science of what is real and what is not once upon a time, but now.'

And we ask them yet to consider it again. For what we use in religion is a science, not a fairy-tale, a science of faith having its own organum of research, our experimental method, the instrument of Verification by Life. You have called us obscurantists. We reply that the appeal to study facts not fancies comes not from you to us only, but from us to you. We ask you to come with us and verify a law unifying all existence, which has written itself on the facts of every order from the movements of man's subtlest intelligence to the dust which quickens into flesh of worm and the fibres which burgeon into flower. Behold, we say, Life: and behold, it is the Mutual Self-giving of creature to Creator, the Sacrifice, the Passion of the Christ.

We ask you to investigate with us not the pages of a record witnessing a far-off event, reputed by us divine; not the pages of past-away thinkers who wrote interpretations of that witness; not these, or not now. No, but to question things that happen in this living hour, the things that happen upon that Self of you, which is all of existence you can with clearness certainly know, upon your mind, your heart, your will; things that are the movings of a Life in you when it thinks, or purposes, or loves and hates. We ask you to question these, with that same science of yours that questions lesser things; as sternly, as patiently, as discerningly; and to abide by the answer that shall come to you. To us has come the answer, that what has lit upon our senses is the Finger of the Reality, that this Reality is known to us by the life which pulses in us on that touch, that this intercourse is the Divine become the Human, the Word made Flesh, which is the Be-All of the Christian's faith. That answer has come to us along the ways of science: we men of faith are scientists in our faith, and say to our brothers in quest 'Come and see what we—not have believed, but have seen.'

And you have called us preachers of asceticism, deniers of the natural life and its wholesome good, calling humanity to take Poverty for bride. But that is not the gospel we are preaching here. Sacrifice is the message, not asceticism: a sacrifice that must receive the answer by fire. Man can live only by giving himself to God: to save a man there must be the Passion. But the Passion is the rendering of the personal self to the infinite Personality, in utter obedience to the All-Will. That Will is that man shall suffer, and also that man shall enjoy: there is a Passion which appoints a fast from pleasures, or even stretches the confessor upon a rack; and there is a Passion which floods his veins with the joy of strength and fires him with the communion which is feast. There is a sacrifice which is the casting away for more unencumbered soldiership of this good or of that —body's comfort, heart's out-going, reason's delight of quest; and there is also the sacrifice which is the glad spending of life's abundance by living at life's height, by rendering the obedience whose service is freedom, whose labour joy, in the delight of prosperous battle for holy cause, in the sweetness of love's fruition, divine or human, in the rapture of the flight of thought, when it soars upon a wing beyond the bound of sense, and across the heaven threshold beholds the Unbeholden in a vision that maketh blest. Both these are sacrifices, the suffering and the bliss, and few are they who are not called to both.

And you say we are pedants in religion, who have

narrowed the life of faith to mere devotionalness, or even to the thin scholarship of theologian or ecclesiastic. We thank you for that reminder. It is not quite unneeded. But when we recollect ourselves, we gladly put aside these professional mannerisms, and are, as you, realists in the study of salvation. We do know, we also, that a way is not a goal, and an art instrument is not an art creation, and a diet is not a health; we know that a creed's rehearsal is not an act of faith, nor a ritual is a worship, nor any mode of religion is religion's self. We can discern, as could the Celtic saint, a brother believer in the man who is not yet of the Church by sacrament or by teaching, yet has 'guarded safe all his life the natural good': nay, we can discern a brother even in one who cannot discern that brotherhood in himself, and names himself unbeliever, yet who walks by the same rule of sacrifice as the brethren walk, and to whom, if he be in some thing otherwise minded, God shall reveal even this in God's true hour.

And you have called us unreal, still echoing the doctrines of original sin and a dying world, and the vanity of works without faith, survivals of a barbarous conscience, while mankind's grown intelligence 'is not worrying about its sins,' and turns to a Deity who on His part is not caring about the contrition of men's heart but about the service of their hand. Again we thank you for the reminder. But those of us for whom sin and salvation are but other names for death and life unto God, do not incur your censure. Our doctrine that sin must be repented and forgiven is but change of language for a doctrine, learned from universal nature and charged with all her realness, that whatever thing would live must live by sacrifice of self, and he that sins has refused that sacrifice and shall forfeit that life.

IX

But let us not make our appeal only to those who concern themselves with Christianity by an interest, friendly or hostile. They are always the few. But the Gospel must be preached to the poor, which means to the many: to the poor, whether their poverty is of material good or of spiritual, the wealth of wit, of imagination, of heart-affluence, of social opportunity. Unless the Gospel which preaches that salvation is life, and life is sacrifice, can appeal to these poor who are the many, it is no Gospel, not even for the few to whom it may have seemed so.

But a Gospel to these it is. It holds the secret which they all are in quest of: it speaks the word which their natures desire each one to utter and have not uttered. Consider them. Among these poor are those whom men call the Rich: the "idle rich," of whom we hear much just now, and the not idle rich, commonly called the Educated, of whom we of this place see more. What is the appeal of this gospel to these?

That it offers them what they are seeking; what they ignorantly worship, this it declares. The one class of rich are believed and believe themselves to be seeking pleasure. Like their congener in old Rome who 'made a feast, drank fierce and fast, and crowned his hair with flowers,' or 'drove abroad in furious guise,' but could by no such means enchant 'the impracticable hours,'—so these. They think it is pleasure they are seeking. They mistake, it is life they are wanting; life of a pulse beating higher, life of sense that quickens and glows, a nerve that thrills more responsively, of a being that expands unconstrained. They are seeking life, but seeking it astray. They will not lure life to them by the deliciousness of a feast, nor overtake her by the fury of their wheels. But our gospel says to them, 'Seek life where it is to be found—in sacrifice; not in selfishness but in sharing, in the giving which is more blessed than receiving, but is a giving and a receiving in one. Seek it where some of your like do seek and do find it; the man of state living laborious days not for self or family or faction but for the commonweal; the man of landed wealth who is master of a dependent flock, but master and pastor in one; the man of business careful for the wealth of his borough, and for its righteousness; the man of communal zeal who nurses the social settlement or fosters the school; the man at arms who gives a gallant self to work the Peace of Britain at an empire's outposts, ruling with selfless care the wild men and his own, their lover and beloved. All these,' says our gospel, 'find life, and pleasure that is life's self-utterance, because they make sacrifice. Seek as these, and ye too shall find.'

X

But those other rich who have the wealth less of gold than of intellectual and social opportunity, is our creed for them? Of some, of many it surely can be said that they too seek life, but amiss, because they seek it in the form of security, not of venture. Venture they decline, sometimes from an ignoble fear of narrowing their comforts, as by encumbering themselves with ties of family in the competitive struggle; sometimes from the less unworthy fear of narrowing their intellectual development, if the attitude of spectator of all time and existence is exchanged for that of actor, or is compromised by definite choice of a creed or of a cause. Each is a mistaken fear. It is nature's law that, if a man will not venture, neither shall he win. And 'enlargement,' says a Hebrew lyrist, 'doth God appoint for walls, and bulwarks'; enlargement, freedom, range, adventure, forthgoingness is the soul's safety, not security that pens it in a rampart. It is by the path of sacrifice in a human sharing of the human struggle, in the 'dear concerns' of wife and child and their daily bread, in the knowledge and love which spring like flowers along that path; it is in succouring a state by the citizen service of rearing a family and entry into affairs, or a church by the churchman service of adhesion to a system, that heart and mind have enlargement and the will has range. Those who fail to lose life thus, fail to find it. They have withheld the sacrifice of adventure, have refused to espouse the bride Reality, austere bride but impassioned; and in their singleness are left barren of a mortal's deed.

XI

And those poor whom men call the poor, will this gospel be hid from them?

What is the deepest cause of the defection of working men from religion? Surely it is that the religion too commonly administered to him is in his eyes not real enough. He will not think the same of the religion of Life. Nothing under heaven has such reality as life. We will then go to him and say: 'Brother, you come but little to our house of prayer, and less to our feast of charity. Our forms of prayer, you say, somehow miss the mark of your actual experience. Our Bible, as certain self-sent pastors of human society tell you, is in part an old almanac and in part a fairy tale. You are wanting bread for yourself and little ones, and the Churches give you a stone, the doctrine of a better life coming in the other world; this does not fill your hunger, and your pastor of society tells you to let be the other world and take this world which is your own by right. Brother, *we* do not counsel you to wait for the world to come, as some Christian guides bid you; nor, as those rival advisers, to clutch the world that now is. We counsel you to love and to seek the two worlds, which are the whole. We call you not to be worldly, not to be other-worldly:

we call you to be whole-worldly. For all the world is before you, as before Dives the millionaire; all things are yours, things present and things to come, as they were Paul's the Apostle; all are yours, because you are a soul of man, and your life is unto all the world that is, since it is life unto God.'

We mean that a soul fulfils its destiny of bliss not by its possessions or its opportunities in a mortal fortune, but according as it is alive to the whole world, which is the eternal. The Christ, whose passion made the eternal fortune of mankind, was man's saviour not because He was teacher, exemplar, even atoner, but because He was a Life, a life unto God, kindled in the flesh of man to kindle all men everywhere; not because He was a man wise, saintly, wonderful beyond measure, but because He was a man wholly alive unto God. That life can become every man's, wherever born, however nurtured, however clothed with knowledge and armed with opportunity. A man, it has been boasted ere now, 'a man's a man for a' that'; and in highest estate or humblest a soul is a soul,— and what know we greater? In this your narrow opportunity on earth, yet see your calling, brother,— to be a man and live : to make your response of soul to its Maker by the hourly sacrifice of self : to feed by your wage the little flock round the scanted board, to be true to the comrade, loyal to the master, of your toils, generous to the poorer than you, generous in heart to the wealthier; to realise your force of manhood in art or craft or craftless labour, to stamp the seal of your person on the clay of a lowly industry, to match the might of a spirit against the weight of earth's brute matter : nay, even to go on discovery of the world-secret, you the unlearned and unleisured, to ride on quest of the Grail as far and fast as the best-mounted chivalry of the learned and rich; to ride and overtake, and one day, O my brother, to find and see; in some shock of sorrow to behold heaven open, in some brief natural joy to taste the Father's love and know how gracious the Lord is, in some sacrament in the dim morning chancel, before the city wakes, to behold the Vision pass that maketh blest, and to know that you the day-workman, you the office drudge, the harried breadwinner, that you have been at the heart of things, have touched the mystery which many prophets and kings desire to touch, and have found the life which we have unto God in Christ.

XII

One last word. To many, and them among the devoutest, it may seem that this claim of Life, as a ground of truth, to have reality, is of all claims the least sustainable. Reality, these will sigh, is just what we miss in it. The historic event of the marvellous Coming and Going Hence of Jesus, the sure word of a Scripture and a Creed guaranteed by this solidity of substance and shape, the structure and unchanging order of the Christian Church, which is the Body, the visible Body, of the Christ,—these have reality : these we can touch and make sure of : these are rock under the feet of our faith. But this Life you speak of, this fugitive, frail, formless consciousness, which writes itself upon the soul in no clear and lasting lettering, but in the music, fleeting and undetainable, of a thrill in the spirit, a glow, a tone, a yearning, an elation,— this to us is a phantasm, 'beautiful but ineffectual,' adding to our faith nothing. We are not mystics asking the angels' food of vision; we are men who live by the bread of fact.

And we answer :—Dear brother and dear sister, if it is hard to realise Life, the reason is a blessed one. The reason is in the greatness of you : greatness of a human soul which has for home a universe that is one and continuous, the robe of Divinity woven without seam throughout, and into all that whole can enter as into an inheritance which in right is already hers and shall be also in possession. By degrees must we inherit. We come to our own by feeling after the unseen eternal facts with a blind, advancing touch of a soul which is her own organ to perceive them, and perceives them by the life and health in her, which is the answering touch of the Unseen Things. A blind advancing touch; blind because it advances, and the new knowledge can never have articulate shape till already we have passed beyond it to knowledge again new. 'Man never is but always to be blest'—with the fruition of the vision of God. This we think is what the mystics are telling us when they declare a faculty of intuition, which is seated in no one of our experiencing senses. But however that may be, you, brother or sister, who complain that this way of knowing God is too frail and dim, are complaining of your high estate, the estate of a finite being that can for ever grow into infiniteness of being. You are murmuring at the lot of the People of God who are forbidden to worship Him by any manner of similitude, any image of Reality graven by the mind's device. That image we shall see, but not now, shall behold but not near. Meanwhile in this our mortality we behold God by a knowledge which is the life that vibrates upon our mortal members from the Unbeholden. Pray we then with Chrysostom, but in altered order of his petitions, that there be granted us in this world the life everlasting and in the world to come the knowledge of God. For so the order of Creation is followed in the order of man's attainment of the divine. In the beginning when God made the heaven and the earth, 'there was evening and there was morning, one day.' Eve and morn were of one stuff of time, parts of one whole: but evening first and then the morning. So is it in the full creating of man. There is the evening twilight of our human intelligence on this side of a night which men call Death. But heaviness of faint knowledge may endure for a night: joy cometh in the morning, the joy of clear vision under the eternal dawn. Ah, yes: even as here and now for one of us some dim and tangled web of thought, which we had carried to our pillow, will stand unravelled and illumined at first touch upon the brain of day, so, as we will guess, the spirit of man shall rouse from its over-night dusk of mere mortal experience into the clear shining of the morrow's intuition. For so God giveth to His beloved—in sleep. 'I will lay me down and sleep,' our soul may tell herself; 'when I wake up I shall be satisfied with His likeness —when I wake.'

www.ingramcontent.com/pod-product-compliance
Lightning Source LLC
Chambersburg PA
CBHW071429150426
43191CB00008B/1089